A Book Lover
in Texas

A Book Lover in Texas

Evelyn Oppenheimer

University of North Texas Press
Denton, Texas

First printed in 1995 in the United States of America

10 9 8 7 6 5 4 3 2 1

The paper in this book meets the minimum requirements of
the American National Standard for Permanence of paper for
Printed Library Materials, z39.48.1984.

Library of Congress Cataloging-in-Publication

Oppenheimer, Evelyn , 1907–
    A book lover in Texas / by Evelyn Oppenheimer.
        p.   cm.
    Includes index.
    ISBN 0-929398-89-0
    1. Literature—Book review.   2. Criticism.   I. Title.
PN51 . 066   1995   94-49021
028. 1 ' 092—dc20   CIP
[B]

Design by Amy Layton

"To write an autobiography as literature is the most difficult thing anyone could do."

—Robert Loomis

"But the Work shall not be lost. For it will appear in a new and more elegant Edition Revised and corrected by the Author."

—Benjamin Franklin's self-written epitaph

"Go litel bok."

—Chaucer, *Troilus and Criseide*

*D*edicated to the memory of my parents and to the great teachers and authors, the friends and audiences through so many years.

Acknowledgments

First to my publisher and editor, Frances Vick of the University of North Texas Press, who ran herd on me until I was in the corral, and also to the Dallas Chapter of the Women's National Book Association for their memorable tribute of honor in November 1994. My appreciation, too, for the special interest Dr. Valerie R. Hotchkiss, Director of Bridwell Library, and her staff have shown in my collection.

Contents

Introduction

The first sentence of Evelyn Oppenheimer's *A Book Lover in Texas* promises humor and vitality and passion. "Listen!" I said to my husband and read the sentence to him. And "Listen!" I said again and again as I read through this fine manuscript. Writing with humor and intelligence, Oppenheimer becomes a poet, an agent, an essayist and a reviewer. Any one of these attest to the rare intelligence that was evidenced throughout her Dallas education and which blazed forth at the University of Chicago.

Oppenheimer is most poetic when she writes about the natural world, calling these all too few passages digressions. In these pages the pace slows; sound and sense come together. Reading her lyrical description of a mountain tree I recall Dorothy Wordsworth's *Journals*, and know that here, too, the reader has encountered the heart and mind of a poet.

As an essayist, she comments on literature, on writers and, astringently, on writers who read from their work. She scoffs at the idea of "regional" writing, and thoughtfully, succinctly, tells why. Her dispassionate, logical passages about the modernity of Shakespeare sent me to my own bookshelves to find and to savor again some favorite passages in *Lear*. At times, her opinions about writers astonish, so accustomed are we to reviewers who tiptoe around major faults in a work with lukewarm praise as if afraid that a negative but honest criticism would "step on a crack, break your mother's back." While one may disagree with her opinions of these writers, one applauds her honesty. There is nothing mean-spirited about her criticism; it never says, "Look at me! See how cleverly, satirically I can write." And when she likes a work, she is unreserved with her praise.

She has written books—books as varied as one would expect from such an intellect: a children's book, biographies, histories, texts, and now, this memoir. These speak to her ability as a book writer far better than I could.

Oppenheimer was the first and, for some time, the only agent in Texas. Her anecdotal stories about agenting make one realize that success in writing owes something to luck as well as craftsmanship.

Evelyn Oppenheimer's career as a reviewer is without parallel. When she had finished her first oral review, she listened to other reviewers and then she carefully redefined the purpose of the oral review and began. As a reviewer she came to know the famous and near famous who visited

Dallas. Her stories about personalities are sometimes funny, often dramatic, always lively. Spanning five decades, she has been read and heard, especially the latter, all over the southwestern part of the United States. While many do not know her face, her style and her voice are cozily familiar to readers and listeners.

Oppenheimer is treasured by bookstores and bookwriters and bookreaders, by librarians and publishers and academics. "Listen!" her book tells us all. And we do. We are. We listen to this woman, this Dallas treasure.

—Jane Roberts Wood
author of *The Train to Estelline, A Place Called Sweet Shrub, Dance a Little Longer* and editor of *Out of Dallas: 14 Short Stories*

The Beginnings

$\mathcal{I}$t all began when I went to bed with King Arthur.

I was six or seven years old, and beside my bed of bird's-eye maple was a bookshelf with my other friends— *The Five Little Peppers and How They Grew, Heidi, Royal Children of English History, Rolf in the Woods, Miss Minerva and William Green Hill, A Child's Garden of Verses, Robin Hood, Black Beauty,* Charles and Mary Lambs' *Tales from Shakespeare, Robinson Crusoe, Ivanhoe, Treasure Island,* and *20,000 Leagues Under the Sea.*

One by one they had come to me as birthday presents, or at Christmas from my mother, or when my father went on business trips to Chicago where he always visited the Marshall Field's book department. Some were gifts from my Swedish governess, Emma Bergman, who taught me to read and know the magic of books. Others

*Evelyn Oppenheimer as an infant with her mother Gertrude
(Courtesy of Evelyn Oppenheimer)*

*Louis Oppenheimer (Courtesy of Evelyn
Oppenheimer)*

came from Dr. Elbert Dunlap who had delivered me and
evidently foresaw my future.

I was an only child, but never lonely. Who could be
lonely in that house at 1619 South Ervay Street with its big
attic and basement and trees to climb and big backyard for
riding my Shetland pony? There was a stable for my pony
and my father's horse, and on Sunday mornings we would
ride south on Ervay to the woods that were still on Park
Row in the First World War days when an army camp was
at Fair Park.

At that time South Dallas was locale for as many fine homes of prominent citizens as were those to the north on Ross Avenue and in Munger Place. On Ervay at South Boulevard were the fine old homes of Simon Linz of the jewelry company, and Gerard Dreyfus, owner of one of the quality menswear stores, among others such as E. M. Kahn, Gus Roos, and Hurst Brothers.

Across the street (and streetcar tracks) from our home was that of Morris Liebman, who with his brother Rudolph owned the Texas Paper Company. Next door was the Buell family of Buell Lumber Company. Next to us was the wife of Henry Pollock who preferred to live downtown over his trunk and luggage store with, as all the gossips knew, his mistress.

In the next block was the home of one of the few general practitioners, Dr. Emil Aronson. Later I would borrow and read all the classical and medical books in his and his son Howard's library, just as I went through the *Rover Boys* and *Tom Swift* series that the Liebmans' sons Walter and Richard had. Variety was the spice of my early literary life, as indeed it has continued to be.

The entertainment value of gossip has always held a "prime time" in society long before that phrase ever was used in television. It has also fed many a novelist. Whispered behind fans, monogrammed handkerchiefs, cigars and pipes, it drifted into the long ears of children more than adults thought possible.

Thus one came to know that the beautiful young wife of a local merchant prince relieved her boredom by enjoying an affair with the Dallas mayor, and bore a son who inherited all His Honor's physical features. In due time the husband shot himself, not too expertly but at least effectively. A similar event of more serious implications occurred when a young Jew married the daughter of a prominent Protestant family who had their "restricted" Dallas Country Club refuse him membership or even admittance. The glitz of Big D society had its shadows then as now.

One heard about soaring cotton prices and the incredible luck of oil wildcatting a few miles away, and a certain young bank president's marital infidelity and the proliferation of a red light district called "The Cribs," whose landlord aspired to the category of "real estate."

In later years when I was lucky enough to acquire copies of the 1895–96 edition of the *Red Book of Dallas* published by Holland Brothers Company—the first Red Book on an urban society in Texas—and the *Blue Book of Dallas* 1909 edition published by the South Company, their content brought back memories of conversations I had heard or overheard between my parents and their friends.

Such books were forerunners of Emily Post and Miss Manners by including in their content the all-important do's and don'ts of shaking hands for ladies and gentlemen (never referred to as men and women, or our inane compromise now of *person*). Also well covered were the proper wording of invitations to various social events and the very definitive use of calling cards on the days when "ladies received."

Especially noted was the disgrace of arriving late at a dinner party. The correct timing was to get there ten minutes *before* the hour designated. I can recall that several couples were infamous for not observing that rule. To mention their names even now might tarnish the reputations of their survivors.

After dark only evening dress was acceptable—formal dress. How my father was tolerated I don't know, as he never owned a tuxedo. Exceptions were made, obviously. Mavericks have always been popular in Texas.

The advertisements in those early books of social directory not only echo many memories among the older generation but are of special interest in revealing that women were very much into business in those early years as dressmakers, milliners, teachers of music and dancing and voice and "miniature painting" and, of course, hairdressers, with their various shops and studios which were all downtown. There were even two ladies selling insurance then.

An ad of special prominence in those early directories extolled a Harry Eeles as "The Practical Horseshoer on Elm Street." There was no ethical hesitation among the handful of doctors and dentists to advertise at that time, and it took a full page ad to laud the multiple benefits of the old Gill Well Bath House on Maple Avenue as "The Carlsbad of America." I can still faintly remember the horrible taste of that Gill Well water when my parents once went to get a bottle of it, a taste much worse than that of the famous Crazy Water at the Mineral Wells resort hotel where they and the Seymour Myers family used to go by train for weekend holidays.

No ad appeared for a most popular and socially approved little park on the edge of town where a draft beer parlor was located. Couples, even families, would drive there in their carriages and discreetly sip the foamy delight with, of course, soda pop for the children. I can vaguely recall going there with my parents in our surrey (no fringe on top) and being allowed one taste of the beer, and in my excitement at such a treat I leaned too far over the carriage and fell out, much to my father's amusement and my mother's despair.

In those World War I days one went with one's mother shopping for delicacies at the grocery and market stores, Craddock's on South Ervay, and Hunt's on North Ervay (forerunners of today's Simon David), and of course for clothes and accessories at Sanger Brothers and A. Harris and Titche-Goettinger and the new Neiman Marcus and for shoes at Volk Bros.

My parents played in a weekly small limit poker game with friends who met in each others' homes. When they met at our house to play around the dining room table, I was sometimes allowed to stay up and watch until 10:00 P.M. when a platter of cold meats and cheese or cake and fruit was served. I remember one such evening when Al Neiman lost in the game to my mother and jovially handed her his keys to the store.

What fun it was at Sanger's to ride up and down that first escalator and to browse in their book department, presided over by Miss Bertha Prager, or to go to that first lending library of Edna Smith's at A. Harris. For our school books we went to Van Winkle's or the Schmalzried second-hand book store, forerunner of the Half Price Book Stores and others in that category so helpful to collectors and to those of us in research as well as avid readers of limited means.

Growing out of the frontier days when circuit-riding Methodist preachers carried religious books in their saddle-bags to the pioneer farm and ranch homes was the great book store of Dallas, Cokesbury's, so named to combine the names of two early bishops, Coke and Asbury. As managed by J. F. "Bliss" Albright, it developed the biggest sales of books in the country, which was quite a shock to folks visiting this hinterland from the east.

In the later years of the 1920s, 1930s and 1940s, there would be the literary rendezvous of Elizabeth Ann McMurray's famous book shop on Commerce Street which was to be one of my radio book review sponsors later on in the 1960s and 1970s. I remember visits there with Sinclair Lewis, Frances Parkinson Keyes, Paul Wellman, Irving Stone, Harnett Kane, etc. When Mrs. Keyes (she pronounced it Kise), author of the bestsellers *River Road, Dinner at Antoine's*, etc., was entertained at an elitist woman's club and served tea, the grande dame of New Orleans literati bellowed out, "Get me a bottle of bourbon!" Hastily the Dallas ladies appointed a committee to rush to a liquor store in one of their Cadillacs and rush back with a bottle of whiskey. The guest of honor became more affable, in fact downright sociable. After a couple of slugs, she glowed.

There was Kay Harper's fine Baker Hotel Book Shop, and for collectors of the rare there was Aldredge's. Never forgotten was the day when I met Eva Le Gallienne at the Baker Book Shop when she was in Dallas for her memorable performance in *Hedda Gabler*.

We also had memorable intervals of opera. As a child I remember going with my mother and father, Gertrude and Louis Oppenheimer, to see and hear *Lohengrin* and *Tosca* at the coliseum in Fair Park, with voices such as Galli-Curci, and Rosa Raisa and Lily Pons. Mother was from Kirksville, Missouri, but she had visited in Cincinnati and St. Louis and heard the best in music in those cities, as well as playing the piano herself. Father was from Chicago and was no stranger to music and theatre there.

Dad was a remarkable man in so many ways. Whereas my mother had an excellent education, he had to leave school when he was thirteen years old, after his father died, and go to work to support his mother and three younger children. The family had come to Ohio from Hesse Darmstadt, Germany, when my father was an infant.

As a boy he dreamed of becoming a doctor, but that dream had to be buried. He worked at various jobs with horses and got the family to Chicago where a sister found work in a millinery store. Dad became a traveling salesman for companies dealing in market supplies such as cutlery, spices, casings for sausages, butcher blocks and coolers for meat storage.

He chose to travel the new territory of the southwest where a growing population meant more meat markets needing equipment. Traveling Texas, Oklahoma, New Mexico, Colorado, and Kansas, he fell in love with the country and saw its vast potential. Sometimes he would travel in the caboose of a freight train, as many salesmen had to do in the 1890s.

His first gift to my mother before they married, the day when William McKinley was elected president in 1900, was a Navajo blanket which I still have and prize. An Indian blanket was a rare sight to a girl in Missouri. Evidently it made a good impression.

He brought his bride to what seemed an outpost to her, the town he saw for its future urban and business promise—Dallas, Texas. He opened the first market supplies company south of the Mason-Dixon Line, the Texas Butchers Supply Company, with a factory to make butcher blocks and meat coolers. He installed the first refrigeration in Sanger Brothers restaurant, and for the flower farm of the famed eccentric multi-millionaire E. H. R. Green, who owned the first automobile in Texas and took Dad for a ride in it.

After five years the young couple had their first baby, who died in infancy, and several years later I was born.

My parents were readers always, and both enjoyed opera and musicals. On summer vacations at the old Chicago Beach Hotel they took me to see and hear *Rose Marie* and *The Student Prince*. It was a good beginning. Out of the great lottery of birth, I was so very lucky.

My way into the world of music was also opened in Oak Grove School in City Park where a music teacher, Miss Wilcox (if she had another name we never knew it), played recordings on an R.C.A. victrola, and then once a year we entered the Music Memory Contests sponsored by Linz Bros. If we could identify the recordings played, we were awarded little gold pins. How we who won them prized them!

I loved walking to school carrying my box lunch, into which by special credit arrangement, I was allowed to add a huge sour pickle from Young's Grocery Store, which was en route just past Rhinelander Pharmacy where I tried not to look at the soda fountain.

Our class went on to Forest Avenue High School and the wonders of Virgil, Cicero, Caesar, Keats, Longfellow, Wordsworth, Shakespeare, Poe, Shelley, Hawthorne, Emerson, and de Maupassant, as well as chemistry, biology, history and the challenge of algebra and geometry. On weekends we cheered our football team (I was a cheerleader) against that hated rival Oak Cliff High, or went to the Palace Theatre to hear the Hyman Charninsky Orchestra and thrill to the movies of Valentino, Wallace Reid, Garbo, Laughton, Gloria Swanson, Nazimava, Theda Bara, the Gish sisters, Chaplin, and others. Such afternoon galas were topped off with ice cream sodas at Nelson Pharmacy next door to Neiman Marcus. There the handsome young Harold Nelson was an added attraction as he served us giggling girls.

Whatever talent I have as a speaker and broadcaster was nurtured initially by our high school debating society, and the time spent winning the state championship and then the interstate debates held in New Orleans. That top honor awarded me there, however, did not include any visit to the French Quarter, not at that so-called "tender age." "*O tempera, O mores!*"

A remarkable thing is that although Forest Avenue High School no longer exists under that name, its graduates remain organized and active, with semiannual dinner parties and social affairs to celebrate a special esprit.

Some Saturdays required a session, as socially prescribed, at Mrs. John Priestly Hart's Dancing School on Pocahontas Street or in the Knights of Columbus Hall on Main Street, so that we would know what to do and how to do it when the time came to get on a ballroom floor.

In the later years of the 1930s and 1940s, deluxe dating was dining and dancing at the rooftop Baker Hotel's Peacock Terrace, featuring Herbie Kay and Dorothy Lamour, or the Adolphus Hotel Century Room with the Phil Harris Band. Also very popular socially was dining at the downtown restaurants, Town and Country and the Golden Pheasant, the latter famed for its French salad dressing which was bottled and sold regionally for a number of years. I can almost taste it now.

I grew up with my father's love for baseball. School and college nurtured football addiction, and of course I caught our Dallas Cowboy fever and remain happily infected. But always my own game has been tennis, which I taught at a girl's camp in Wisconsin one long hot summer, a stint which in no way qualified me for Wimbledon.

My religious education was directed by my mother's sense of identity. Her father had been a rabbinical student before coming to Missouri as a young man from Mannheim, Germany. Very simply, I was taught who and what I was— a Jewess. However, that never interfered with the child-hood joy I was given in Santa Claus or hunting Easter eggs among the violet beds in our front yard.

The High Holy Days of Rosh Hashanah and Yom Kippur were observed in our home, but in no orthodox fashion. I was taken to Sunday School at the reform Temple Emanu-El and learned very little, unfortunately, for at that time the teachers were untrained volunteers. I was confirmed by Rabbi David Lefkowitz whose personal blessing I never forgot.

Much more education in Judaism came later from the sermons of Rabbi Gerald Klein, and while in Chicago at the university, the sermons of Rabbi Louis Mann and Rabbi Solomon Freehof whose reform temples I attended with friends there. But I learned most from my own reading and the courses in comparative religion taught by Dr. Eustace Hayden at the University of Chicago.

I like best to say my prayers where there are no four walls around me, and I like to think that David wrote his great poetry of the Psalms out in the open of desert and hills or shore where winds and waves speak in their own God-created rhythm.

My parents had a very big surprise for me between high school and college. They had met a woman named Della Mohr who was related to their friends the Emil Stern family. Her specialty was taking small groups to Europe for the traditional Grand Tour. Before I knew it, this teenager was on the SS *Rotterdam* sailing out of New York Harbor.

Under the expert guidance of that teacher from Alabama who had spent so much time and study abroad, we traveled all summer in England, Scotland, France, Switzerland, Italy, and Austria. Even then I avoided going into Germany, as memory was still fresh about the barbarism of Kaiser Wilhelm's army in Belgium, a forerunner of what would come a decade later in the horrors of the holocaust. Austria, too, can leave a taste of bitterness which all the whipped cream and chocolate cannot cover, especially in Vienna where some of us can still hear the sound of the locking of ghetto gates at sunset under the melodic flow of Strauss waltzes.

On that trip I grew up in many ways, but little did I know that our young Italian escort in Rome who gave me the pin off his uniform coat lapel was giving me the insignia of the Fascists. We knew nothing of its real significance then. I doubt if he did either. I still have the pin, a souvenir of sorts.

All that mattered was the great experience of actually being where most of our literature had come from originally, especially England and France. To stand at Stratford by those sculptures of Hamlet and Lady Macbeth and Falstaff and Prince Hal, to stroll beside the swans drifting on the River Avon, just to be in Stratford or in the Lake Country, or to walk along the book stalls by the Seine or to look into the bronze face of the Victor Hugo statue and see all the faces of *Les Misérables*, such an experience is to enter literary heaven.

There would be other trips abroad in later years, most memorably one in 1956 when last minute planning extended our time in Rome and Naples so that a friend and I changed reservations from the ill-fated *Andrea Doria* to a week later, sailing home on the *Cristoforo Colombo,* which saved our lives. But that first trip was the perfect launch into college.

My generation of high school graduates in Dallas were fully prepared to take college entrance examinations, and in most cases, pass them and qualify for any of the top level colleges or universities.

My first choice was Columbia University, but unfortunately I did not know that it, like too many other eastern educational institutions, enforced a quota system for Jewish students. Accordingly, when I got there I was informed by the head of the admission office that I had met all the standards but could not be admitted because their quota for Jews was filled. Then she went behind her desk and tore up my examination papers to remove evidence.

After the shock of that first personal encounter with anti-Semitic prejudice and discrimination where one as naive as I was then would least expect it, I immediately shifted to the University of Chicago where scholarship was all that mattered. The midwest was America, like our southwest. The Fates had dealt me a blow but then gave me a rose, one of finest silver as in *Der Rosenkavalier.*

I soon learned that Chicago in the late 1920s and early 1930s, not New York, was the capitol of literary America.

There on the shore of Lake Michigan were Harriet Monroe and her famed *Poetry Journal*, Carl Sandburg, Theodore Dreiser, Sherwood Anderson, Vachel Lindsay, among others, and at the University of Chicago was the thrilling stimulus of study under Thornton Wilder, Robert Morss Lovett, Teddy Lynn, T. V. Smith, Eustace Hayden, Franz Boas, and, of course, Robert Hutchins, who ignited the Great Books excitement.

On weekends there were student-rate tickets for the top balcony (peanut roost) at the Chicago Symphony. Under the baton of Frederick Stock we could hear the young Horowitz, Heifitz, Kreisler, Menuhin. When affordable for your date, there was the Aragon Ballroom where Wayne King the Waltz King, Guy Lombardo and Ben Bernie played. Affordable at times was a liverwurst sandwich on rye at the Red Star Inn on the near north side. Always and best of all were the walks in the snow on campus after study at night in the great library.

To one who had never before known the long months of winter wonderland, that sense of silent serenity and beauty cast a spell of otherworldliness. All urban ugliness disappeared. Everything man-made had its substance merely etched. The campus became a bride gowned in white for purity, and we all became poets in boots and galoshes.

During those college days I began reviewing books for Chicago newspapers, the *Post* and the *Journal*. Some of us university students made a few dollars that way, but the thrill was to see your name in print for the first time, though

I had done some high school reporting for the *Dallas Times Herald* at home.

Llewelyn Jones was the famed book critic of the *Chicago Post*, and to have reviews accepted by him was no little honor, but a girl went in and out of his office to select a book or deliver a review at her own risk. Speed and ingenuity were requisite to escape what today is the sexual harassment situation and issue. Then, we brushed it off as a momentary annoyance and just laughed at the old fellow.

One of the first reviews I wrote for the *Post* was of the brilliant novel *The Fountain* by British writer Charles Morgan, a bestseller from Knopf in 1932. I was also assigned some special feature stories, notably to interview Samuel Goldwyn on one of his visits to Chicago. In a state of nerves I was escorted to his hotel suite and saw the all-powerful Hollywood mogul, famous for his verbal gaffes, slumped at a desk, his short legs up on the desk, his head back against the chair, his eyes closed. I sat down and waited for him to wake up, but his eyes opened and he looked at me and said in his heavy accent, "You sink I am seeping, but I am sinking and sinking and sinking. Do you want to know what I am sinking about?"

I assured him that was why I was there—to know what he was thinking about. There never was an easier interview, and, to the editor's surprise, I wrote a story as good as their regular reporter could have done if he had been available. The editor, however, did not push his luck and neither did I. I went back to book reviewing.

I also worked part-time at a downtown book shop called Walden's (no connection with the current chain), where the "salary" was mainly a discount on the books I wanted to buy—the latest Millay or Edgar Lee Masters or Richard Aldington or Sinclair Lewis or Dorothy Parker or Theodore Dreiser. . . .

Perhaps most important was being given my first radio by a friend when I was recovering from an emergency appendicitis operation. Little did I know then how important that new wonder would be to and for me in a few years. Of most interest to me was the New York critic Alexander Woollcott broadcasting his astute and acid wit about books and authors on the air. I listened whenever I could and began a dream—for books for people—not just newspaper readers.

As we who are alumni and alumnae know, the University of Chicago was, and is, a state of mind unique in academia. Even as a freshman there I was aware of not being *taught* as much as being inspired and stimulated to think and learn. That difference is great and of lasting effect. It was living the words of Walter Pater of a century before, "Not to burn with that hard gemlike flame is to sleep before evening." I recall my first day's class with the great teacher of English literature, Teddy Lynn, famous for his unorthodox approach.

He looked over the crowded classroom in old Cobb Hall, his bright blue eyes sparking under bushy brows, and he barked out the question, "Why are you here?" This lowly Texas novitiate felt her hand go up on some kind of reflex, and I said, "We are here to be and study with men like you." His answer as he fixed his eyes on me was, "Well, I'll be damned."

As class ended he signaled me to stay. He wanted to know where I was from. When I told him Texas, he gave me his first smile and said, "I thought so."

Professor Lynn was from the days when only a bachelor's degree was essential for a university faculty, well before the Ph.D. epidemic.

At the University of Chicago I had the feeling that I was at a gourmet cafeteria, with every field of study irresistible. I took all the undergraduate courses in anthropology, and dreamed of becoming an archaeologist for treasures of knowledge of the past, like the great Franz Boas who came to lecture at the developing Field Museum of Natural History and which our class attended.

But my fascination was with philosophy as taught by the noted T. V. Smith, a veritable Niagara of wit and scholarship. He was a fellow Texan, born on a poor cotton farm in Brown County near Blanket in 1890. Tall, skinny, freckled, sandy-haired, he had walked barefooted to the University of Texas in Austin to work his way through college. He literally lived in the library between jobs and classes. The brilliance of his record there catapulted him to the University of Chicago for a doctorate degree and then as professor of philosophy from 1923 to 1948.

In the classic Greek tradition the philosopher included the study of politics, otherwise we would never have had the guidelines of Plato's *Republic*. Thomas Vernor Smith became an Illinois State Senator and then was elected to the United States Congress as a Democrat. There his series of debates with Senator Taft produced books defining the Texan's horizon-wide concept of democracy. Between legislative sessions he continued teaching, and in one of his classes assigned us to write a term paper on any modern American philosopher we chose. I was the only one who chose the idealist of Harvard, Josiah Royce. Across the top page with its "A" grade, Smith wrote to me, "Dear protagonist of the dead Gods." How right he was.

In later years after serving in Italy in the Second World War Smith went to Syracuse University as professor of poetry, philosophy and politics from 1948 to 1956, when he retired to continue his writing. He returned briefly to Texas but his life ended in a nursing home in Hyattsville, Maryland in May, 1964. He was 74 years old or young. I cherish a note from him dated October 15, 1938, "Well do I remember you, dear Lady. Best of all is the good news that your own influence is growing steadily. We teachers (and politicians) must live in our associates, you know." When one is still very young and is called "Dear Lady" by one of America's great scholars, one hugs that to the heart as I did.

All four years on that campus I was in a state of euphoria, drunk with the excitement of learning. The only sad day was when the young president, Robert Hutchins, handed me my diploma in Rockefeller Chapel, with a smile and a compliment on my election to Phi Beta Kappa. I hated the thought of leaving that world of ivy that kept our heritage forever green. The honor of Phi Beta Kappa was to me a small repayment to my parents for the opportunity they had given me, and that was what I tried to say in the telegram that I sent them.

One telegraphed then; long distance phoning was limited to dire emergencies, usually something fatal, and I did not like to call collect. I also liked to save my fifty-dollar monthly allowance to buy books, of course. Then, too, there was a little deli down the street from the dormitory where after study at night we could go and get those liver sausage sandwiches and milk shakes which were the food fashion then before the burgers-fries-coke-hot dogs-pizza era.

About once a month my mother would send a box of chocolate cake and cans of my favorite—white asparagus. What a feast!

The honor system worked to perfection at Chicago. Nobody checked our dormitory goings and comings. Your grades told the tale, and if you were foolish you eliminated yourself. We were assumed to be decent, intelligent adults if we were there.

The university had fraternities but no sororities. However, a group of Chicago girls had formed one, purely social. After my freshman year I was invited to join and to write an initiation ceremony. I produced a humdinger all about eternal loyalty with background music from a recording of the "Meditation" from *Thais*. We all cried and had a wonderful time.

Quite a few years later, 1972 in fact, Muriel Beadle, wife of Dr. George Beadle the eminent geneticist and president of the University of Chicago from 1961 to 1968, wrote a marvelous book entitled *Where Has All the Ivy Gone?*, published by Doubleday. I gave her my Award

Certificate for the best memoir for that year. (More about those awards later.) In a letter dated January 16, 1973, she wrote me, "I am especially pleased by this honor because it indicates that you do not—and correctly in my opinion—consider the book of mainly parochial interest but with affiliation anywhere in the country. Certainly those cities where your book reviews are broadcast have some of the same urban problems that plague Chicago, and all of them are sites of colleges and universities. So very many thanks. . . ."

Those 1960s that she was referring to were indeed difficult for every institution of learning where the ivy of tradition grew, its multiple meanings unperceived by "the flower children." Flowers come and go; ivy endures.

2

Home Again

When the time came for me to return home from Chicago, I remembered that Carl Sandburg had once said that Dallas had the worst newspaper coverage of books in the country. I found that not quite true. Maybe he had based that comment on the page in *The Dallas Morning News* when it was edited by Dr. John McGinnis of Southern Methodist University, who contended that nothing written after 1900 was worth his time. The professor was, of course, entitled to his opinion, but he certainly missed some very good reading.

Fortunately he was succeeded by Lon Tinkle and later Allen Maxwell, both also of Southern Methodist University, and then book reviewing in *The Dallas Morning News* rose to a level of notable quality and was nationally recognized. Today Robert Compton carries on a consistently high standard.

For too long, however, reviewers continued to project in various ways the conviction that literature in Texas began and ended with the sanctified trinity of Dobie, Webb and Bedichek. It was a lingering obeisance that also influenced the young Texas Institute of Letters. Not that those pioneer literati deserved less respect, but new writers of quality who were then emerging such as Mary Lasswell, John Lomax, George Sessions Perry, J. Evetts Haley, David Westheimer, Benjamin Capps, Loula Grace Erdman, Fred Gipson, and others, merited more attention and recognition. Gradually, some reparations of that lack of recognition were made with awards.

The Institute invited their chosen few to join them in membership. Despite my work with and for books throughout Texas, I was not among them until in the mid-1970s when Dr. Decherd Turner (director then of Bridwell Library at Southern Methodist University) insisted upon nominating me for membership and then insisted on my accepting it. I did, and have watched the inner circle perpetuate their mutual admiration society. New blood has seeped in very slowly, all too slowly. Of course, the same is true of most organizations, including Congress and our state legislatures. The future, however, always holds hope for change for the better. But writers are seldom friendly with each other if they work in the same genre or unless they are so well established that they can afford to be friendly, maybe even helpful. Jealousy is an old virus, very old.

The evening paper in Dallas, the *Times Herald*, which went out of existence in December 1991, had a succession

Post cards that were mailed to advertise reviews at Titche-Goettinger's in 1938, signed "most sincerely, Evelyn Oppenheimer" with the title "Dean of Book Reviewers in the Southwest." (Courtesy of Evelyn Oppenheimer)

Publicity photographs of Evelyn Oppenheimer used throughout
her career.

of very interesting and highly qualified book review editors
less bound to the old buddy system. They were Kenneth
Rockwell, playwright and historian John William Rogers,
author Luise Putcamp, Jr., Decherd Turner, Jeff Unger,
and A. C. Greene.

Rogers, a Dallas native and Dartmouth alumnus, had
formerly been book editor of Marshall Field's *Chicago Sun*,
and his plays *Judge Lynch* (which took the Dallas Little
Theatre to New York to win the Belasco National Award),
Roam Though I May and *Where the Deer and the Antelope
Play* had production and publication. One wonders why
they have not been revived by local and regional theatres.
He also wrote one of the best of all books on Dallas history,
The Lusty Texans of Dallas, a collector's item now.

He and I were friends, and often he would bring
camellias from his garden to my mother and me. As he also
was music and theatre critic for the *Times Herald*, it was
always of special interest to read his reviews of those events
in juxtaposition to the coverage by the brilliant *Morning
News* critic, John Rosenfield, famous as the cultural czar of
Dallas, who could make or break any celebrity who came
to the city.

Rosenfield and I were also friends, as our families had
been, and I always urged and hoped that his widow would
collect and edit his newspaper columns before her death.
Alas, that was not done. His major achievement was in
getting the city's moneyed society to back Margo Jones and
the initiation of her theatre-in-the-round. He also supported
Antal Dorati in bringing the Dallas Symphony to a level of
excellence it has never surpassed.

It was a time of newspaper competition in quality. Something else was budding in Dallas, however, as the dozens of women's clubs and church organizations wanted programs of oral book reviews, a new form of entertainment which had come eastward from California.

When I had come home in the mid-1930s to be with my parents, I wondered what I would do besides writing book reviews for the local papers. Then I found a literary oasis at the Civic Federation, a community cultural project directed by Elmer Scott with the support of leaders such as Dr. Umphrey Lee of Southern Methodist University, J. K. Hexter, and Karl Hoblitzelle. Housed in an old home at 1419 Maple Avenue, the lectures and forum discussions there were memorable. Scott brought to Dallas such outstanding and controversial writers and thinkers as Bertrand Russell and Max Eastman. There, too, the great Dr. Robert Raible conducted his Unitarian Church services on Sunday mornings, many of which I attended. That creation of Elmer Scott's was to be equaled only by Eli Sanger's Civic Music Society at Southern Methodist University's McFarlin Auditorium.

Soon I was asked to present several programs in a well-attended series of literary lectures sponsored by the Melrose Hotel and arranged by their social director, a Mrs. Nina Harrell. I recall that one of my lectures was on the great French novel *Jean Christophe* by Nobel Prize winner Romain Rolland, which expanded and dramatized his biography of Beethoven into the life story of a musical genius in the turn-of-the-century world. Nobody in the audience had ever read it in its original ten volumes, but at least a few persons promised a trip to the library. That was worth everything to me.

The first organization to engage me for an oral book review was the Dallas Temple Emanu-El chapter of the Council of Jewish Women, and their request was for no less than Eugene O'Neill's *Mourning Becomes Electra*. I prepared what I thought was the way to do it—adapting a professional review into an entertaining lecture form.

The reaction of the audience was most interesting. The ladies either liked it or very much disliked it as something they were not used to hearing. The latter was of most interest to me, and I went to hear some of those other review programs and was appalled at what I heard and saw.

With all too few exceptions, such as Mrs. Roscoe Bates and Mrs. V. Y. Rejebian, they were *not* reviewers but merely storytellers and amateur actresses of little or no educational background, who in no way stimulated anyone to read the books they "reviewed." What I did see was that this held the potential for a new form of oral reviewing, which, if properly and professionally done, could get many more people interested in reading books than the minority who read newspaper reviews. And so I found my métier— and my future.

The first thing to do was to define the differences between a written review and an oral review, one to be read and one to be spoken and heard. When you read you can stop and think and reread. Obviously you cannot do that when you only listen. Listening, being attentive by ear, can also be tiring. You can only absorb so much within a limited time, a fact that the dear clergy often fail to realize. Ergo, the reviewer should observe a definite time limit. When someone in the audience tells a speaker, "I wish you had gone on another hour," be thankful for the compliment but *never* believe it.

The written review for newspaper or magazine can be entirely critical. Not so in the oral review. If it's negative, it's not entertainment. If the book is so bad, why waste time talking about it? Why give publicity to poor work? Let that be the author's and publisher's problems; they deserve it. Your very selection of a book to review is a statement of its worth.

I saw too that the oral review should do a double job. First it should stimulate interest in reading the book, and it should also further the interpretation and understanding of it for those who have read it, if there is more than mere plot. The reason for this is that in every audience, excepting study groups or classes, a minority have read the book and a majority have not. Accordingly, there must be something of value for both. *Never* should all the story or content be told, for that destroys the purpose of the book. It is written to be *read*. Appalling to me too was the way some so-called reviewers thought of themselves as actresses and dramatized a novel's dialogue.

As I began formulating guidelines for this new profession to serve and promote good books, I put them into practice in the review programs for various clubs in Dallas in the late 1930s. Women who had been used to tea cakes enjoyed getting something more substantial. I remember from that time reviewing the big historical novel, *Anthony Adverse* by Hervey Allen, and the tender little novel *Goodbye, Mr. Chips* by James Hilton that expanded the mind and warmed the heart.

It was a good time for books, those Great Depression and post-Depression years. Books were the best and cheapest entertainment. New novels sold for from one dollar and fifty cents to five dollars. People read, and a boon to all readers was the incomparable series of classics in every category of literature called The Modern Library, well-bound and well-printed and priced originally at only ninety-five cents per book. Yes, once upon a time there were "good old days" in our American publishing. Thus, for a dollar you could get a great book and an apple or roll or mug of coffee—no tax.

In both fiction and nonfiction there were authors producing the highest quality in their various genres: Pearl Buck, Edna Ferber, A. J. Cronin, Louis Bromfield, Daphne du Maurier, Rachel Field, John Steinbeck, Howard Spring, Rebecca West, Thomas Wolfe, Edith Wharton, Sinclair Lewis, John Galsworthy, Emil Ludwig, Will Durant, Margaret Ayer Barnes, Thornton Wilder, Phyllis Bentley, James Truslow Adams, Isak Dinesen, James Hilton, Vincent Sheean, Ellen Glasgow, John Gunther, Marjorie Rawlings, Carl Van Doren, Margaret Armstrong, John Marquand, Christopher Morley, Sholem Asch, Kenneth Roberts, Mary Ellen Chase, William Saroyan, Richard Wright,

James Baldwin. . . . What a reading list to go back to at the
library or in reprints or a used bookstore now.

There was no literary Depression. The climax of that
decade of the 1930s came in 1936 when gold was discov-
ered by the Macmillan Company in Atlanta, Georgia,
where a woman named Margaret Mitchell had an historical novel of masterly narrative art, *Gone With the Wind*.

For some time I had been thinking that book review
programs so popular with clubs should not be limited to
those exclusive memberships. Dallas has always been a
club-y town, the more exclusive the better. In that 1895 *Red
Book* only seven clubs were listed with their members.
Evidently you were in one of them or you were out al-
together, but a listing fourteen years later showed that those
who were "out" began forming and getting into clubs of
their own of various sorts, and the number multiplied over
and over until today's plethora.

Not to be a member of something now is to arouse
suspicion as to just what is the matter with you. The
"organization man," as William Whyte wrote about in his
1956 book, has bred the organization woman of today.
Alas, I am not comfortable in that category. In fact, if one
is not sitting on some kind of committee or board now, one
is branded with far worse than the "Scarlet Letter" of
Hawthorne's time. Of course, that old "Scarlet Letter" has
long since faded away and become invisible in current
literature.

I took my idea of making book review programs
available to the general public, and thereby promoting

books and reading on a much larger scale, to Mr. E. P. Simmons, president of Sanger's at that time, as I knew they had an upper floor auditorium which could seat a couple of hundred people. The idea appealed to him as a new way to attract people into the store (there was only one Sanger store then, on its original site where El Centro Community College is now). Sanger's ran several newspaper ads about the new event, and the book I chose to review, the fine novel *The Last Puritan* by Harvard professor of philosophy George Santayana. We had a capacity audience.

The next month I reviewed the classic Rostand play *Cyrano de Bergerac*, as the following week the great actor Walter Hampden was bringing the play to Dallas. Again we had a full house.

At the upper end of downtown was the Titche-Goettinger department store with a top floor auditorium more than double the capacity of Sanger's. I went there next, and to the great satisfaction of Mr. W. J. Brown, president, and Mr. Milton Pandres, advertising manager, my review programs went on a weekly schedule and filled *their* auditorium.

Women would drive in from a hundred-or-more-miles radius, from towns such as Tyler, Waco, Sherman, Denton, Greenville, Fort Worth, and others, to attend the program, have lunch, do their shopping and return home. The auditorium was enlarged to a seating capacity of six hundred, and when that became standing room only, we began repeating the programs. That put the schedule on a twice a week basis. Then came requests from business and

professional women and *men* for reviews on Saturday and
a week-night, when the store was open as it was in the war
years of 1941–45.

I came to prefer those mixed audiences of both men
and women and still do for the broader scope of interest
and range of reaction. Only with such an audience of high
school students can there be a bit of difficulty. I recall one
such audience where at the mention of anything pertaining
to sex in the book being reviewed, I could hear a wave of
whispers and giggles. I just stopped and said that I had
assumed I was talking to adults, and at once the noise
stopped so that I could go on. However, another audience
of high school Latin students in the east Texas town of
Henderson was as attentive and sophisticated as any I ever
had. Evidently Roman worldliness can still be imported
and imparted by a teacher as fine as Miss Belle Gould was.

When I introduced *Gone With the Wind*, the first
review in Texas to acclaim its literary as well as historical
merit, popular demand reached an all-time high. I presented over a hundred review programs of *Gone With the
Wind* for various organizations locally, throughout Texas
and adjoining states. The publisher sent press clippings of
this phenomenal record to Margaret Mitchell, who wrote
me from Atlanta, Georgia, on October 1, 1936:

> Your letter and the enclosed clippings pleased
> me so very much and made me so very proud.
> It seems almost incredible to me that so many
> people should want to hear about "Gone With

the Wind"! I am especially happy that your city was the scene of these extraordinary events, for I wanted Southern people to like my book. That means more to me than praise from other noted critics in other sections. I cannot thank you enough for letting me know about it. However, I cannot believe that the enormous crowds were entirely due to "Gone With the Wind." You must be a marvelous reviewer, for it takes both high intelligence and charm and personality to draw such large crowds, regardless of what the subject matter of the lecture may be.

I only wished that Rhett or Ashley could have delivered it, personally of course.

Inevitably, Titche-Goettinger developed a book department with Mr. Marvin Steakley as manager. Later, in 1973, he brought Alistair Cooke for a major autographing event of the bestseller *Alistair Cooke's America*. The affair was significant because it drew the largest crowd ever to attend a book autographing in the state at that time, and a thousand books were sold. One man's order for 200 had to be turned down in order to accommodate other persons. Later that day I interviewed the exhausted Mr. Cooke on the municipal radio station WRR-FM. He saw my review copy of his book and reached for it to sign with a pen running out of ink.

He told Mr. Steakley and me of his visit to the White House to interview President Lyndon Johnson, under critical attack then for the Viet Nam shambles. But when the president heard that Cooke and his wife had gone to the Big Bend National Park, he kept the conversation on the wonders of Texas, and Cooke's time was up and he was escorted out before he could even mention the ill-fated war.

No one could have been more pleasant, but despite Cooke's American citizenship, there was still the British coolness or sense of detachment, friendly but within limits—the diplomat.

Reaction in certain quarters to the success of those first public book reviews was interesting. In Washington, D. C., the east Texas congressman Martin Dies blasted me in the Congressional Record for reviewing Jan Valtin's novel *Out of the Night,* and John Roy Carlson's *Under Cover,* exposing Nazi and Communist sabotage in our country. Some persons chose not to believe the report of William Shirer in *Berlin Diary* in 1941, perhaps the same ones who made Hitler's *Mein Kampf* a bestseller in 1939 and who even today contend that the holocaust never happened.

Local newspaper reviewers looked down their noses at the program's popularity. How could a girl just out of college sneak into their backyard and play hardball? They were politely hostile, mainly from jealousy, it would seem. However, when any of them wrote a book of their own, as several did, they sent me a copy for a review and became noticeably more polite and less hostile. It was amusing. Of course, if the book was good I reviewed it, and if it wasn't, I didn't.

Bigger minds were appreciative as, for example, the great Margo Jones of theatre-in-the-round fame. When she brought Tennessee Williams to Dallas for her production of his *Summer and Smoke* in 1947 and I reviewed his *Glass Menagerie*, she was in the front row of my audience.

More and more clubs, schools and church organizations in other cities and towns contacted me for book review programs. I was traveling from Texarkana and Shreveport, Louisiana, on the east, across all of Texas westward to Lubbock, Amarillo, Pecos, Plainview, and Clovis, New Mexico. In between were Midland, Odessa, Abilene, Wichita Falls. From north Texas and Oklahoma my book trail went south to Waco, Austin, San Antonio, Houston—with programs at the historic Shamrock Hotel—Beaumont, Corpus Christi, and McAllen on the border in the citrus valley where I would get orchard-fresh grapefruit to bring home.

Many of those trips were made by train, the old Cotton Belt going east, the Texas and Pacific and the Burlington going west. So very useful too was the Texas Electric Railway, the interurban line which ran from Denison and Sherman through Dallas to Waco, with stops at all towns between and which, regrettably, was terminated in 1956. Then there were the Greyhound buses and my own car with a driver. At first my mother traveled with me, but after my father was stricken in 1941, I had to go alone.

After selling our Ervay Street home our family had moved into the Melrose Apartment Hotel on Oak Lawn at

Cedar Springs in North Dallas, and from the garage there I hired a black employee we knew as driver for trips to small towns not too distant. On one such trip to present a program at a town southwest of Fort Worth in Comanche County, I had a horribly memorable experience when the sponsors of the program refused to let my black driver buy any food and threatened his life if he were there after sunset. I took my dinner out to the car to share with George, locked him in the car, fulfilled my contract to give the program, announced that for no amount of money would I ever return, and we drove back home all that night to safety and some semblance of civilization.

The same shameful situation existed to the east of Dallas in Van Zandt County. However, such disgraceful racism was not limited to rural areas or small towns. I recall only too well the pain I felt when one of the greatest singers of this or any other century, Marian Anderson, came to Dallas and was denied lodging in every hotel in the city and was finally housed in a private home. The great dream of Martin Luther King, Jr., and many others of us was still quite a few years away.

Without any doubt the most peculiar situation I ever encountered in giving book reviews was when I was engaged by a Dallas woman to present my review of Vera Brittain's very fine novel of an English wife trapped in a miserable marriage and unable to get a divorce. The title held perfect irony, *Honourable Estate*. I naturally assumed that the program was to entertain her club or a social party. However, when I drove to her mansion in a deluxe residential area, I was amazed to see no cars parked there. Had I made an error in date and time?

No. The lady met me at the door and took me into a huge living room. One person was seated there, a man, her husband. He was the audience. I had contracted to give the program, and somehow I managed to review the book. Never was I more uncomfortable, nor did the check, a glass of wine and caviar canapé make me feel any better. Several months later I heard of their divorce.

I came under fire for being the only reviewer in Texas to defend the validity of Edna Ferber's novel *Giant*. After all, I had met some similar characters. Louise Thomas, the Doubleday director of promotion, wrote on October 29, 1952:

> You certainly have done some wonderful work on "Giant," and we are all so grateful. Miss Ferber has been very impressed with your articulate reviewing which has had a great deal of influence on sales of the book.
>
> I hope very much that the *Saturday Review* will reprint your script, and I am urging them to do so. Their review certainly took the book less than seriously.
>
> You are doing a grand job for *all* books. More power to you.

The greatest trepidation I recall facing at that time was when I reviewed the Sholem Asch novel *The Nazarene*.

Billie Billingsley (left) and Evelyn aboard the Cristoforo
Colombo *in 1956, taken at Napoli. A last minute change of
plans put them on this ship rather than the ill-fated* Andrea
Doria. *(Courtesy of Evelyn Oppenheimer)*

What if some crank fanatic in a public audience would
begin heckling a Jewess reviewing a Jewish scholar's
portrayal and interpretation of the life and teaching of
Jesus? My fears proved groundless. I reviewed the book
many times without any such incident occurring. It's good
to be able to report that from the so-called Bible Belt.

An especially memorable program affair was the one
arranged and presented in Austin by the gracious and
lovely Mrs. Allan Shivers, wife of the governor at that time,
for my review of Tom Lea's classic history *The King Ranch*.
I had attended the inaugural reception and ball for the

Shivers when he was elected governor in 1950 and have never forgotten the charm of the governor and Marialice. It was a moment of valid elegance, an unsung Camelot.

In Austin a most interesting contact and friendship developed with the outstanding art restorationist, collector and dealer there, Dewey Bradford. A character of rare wit and knowledge of the art and book worlds, he had rescued the artist Salinas from the gutter and nursed him into more production of his fine work. Famed for his "Country Store" collection of pictures and books, much of which he loaned to various governors for display in the Governor's Mansion, Bradford also gave Lyndon Johnson a hiding place in his home after the infamous Duval County voting episode in 1948. That fact has never been mentioned and is presumably unknown by the various biographers of Lyndon Johnson. When I visited Dewey and his wife Josephine in their treasure-filled home on the cliffside road above Barton Springs, we would stroll and sit out on the patio terrace overlooking the Colorado River and the not too distant capitol. It was there that he gleefully confided his story about his one-time political refugee.

In a letter of February 8, 1961, when he was vice president, Mr. Johnson wrote to me about the possible use of my book review broadcasts for the U. S. Information Agency, and in it he included, "It has been quite some time since we met through Dewey and Jo Bradford, but I hope the time is not too far distant when we could meet again . . . ." A month later, March 10, 1961, a letter came from Edward R. Murrow of the U.S.I.A. suggesting that I send a tape to Voice of America for foreign re-broadcast of some of my reviews, which of course I was glad to contribute.

It was Dewey Bradford who arranged for me to act as agent for artist Peter Hurd to paint the mural in the Lorenzo de Zavala State Archives and Library in Austin. During that time a friend and I had the pleasure of visiting Hurd and his wife, Henriette Wyeth, at their ranch in San Patricio, New Mexico. His parting gift was a big box of the most delicious apples from his orchard. Today, prints of one of the Hurd landscapes with the ever-present windmill, and also his incomparable portrait of the old vaquero praying for rain, are on the walls of my library.

There is a museum gallery at the Hurd's Sentinel Ranch and also a museum in Roswell exhibiting their art. Too few know of Henriette Wyeth Hurd's exquisite work in still life at the Roswell Museum, and also a nude even more beautiful than her brother Andrew's much publicized Helga.

Peter was a fascinating man of multiple talents, from his art to polo and horticulture—especially orchids. I never knew a person who so completely identified himself with the land he loved. He knew where he was most himself, and that was there in that New Mexico valley on the Rio Hondo where he could capture the beauty of sky and land that the moods and drama of nature reveal. But he cherished the written word too and we had many good talks infused with his insights and sense of humor. A warm-hearted man, he was more out-going than the quiet, reclusive Henriette who stayed more within her art. They

Photograph of Paul Horgan and Peter Hurd at Sentinel Ranch, San Patricio, New Mexico. (DeGolyer Library, Southern Methodist University DeGolyer Exhibits, "The Collector's Eye" p.30, item 68.)

were a remarkable couple in their understanding of each other.

For years I urged Peter to write an autobiography which, alas, he never did, though he contracted with me to be his agent for it on February 4, 1961, just as there was a contract for the Austin mural March 17, 1961, with me as agent. However, he had his son-in-law Peter Rogers complete that great mural in Austin. As he wrote in one of his letters to me, "I live in the heart of Mañana land."

Our personal correspondence and contracts have been placed in the De Golyer Library Special Collections at Southern Methodist University. On February 5, 1960, Peter wrote:

> There is absolutely no excuse for not writing about the book you so kindly sent me. My apology for not thanking you long before this. I have read "The Sea Around Us" and now the second book by Rachel Carson is by my bedside to be read.
>
> My reaction to your idea of writing a book is of much interest—only thing is it will have to be a long time process because I have resolved to make my painting primary. I feel I have in recent years let valuable time slip by in other pursuits like the running of this ranch. But I am aware that the sand is running out and I better get busy. Still, the idea of a book has been in the back of my mind for a long time. I would definitely like it to be a worthwhile and really

thinking work, not just another book of memoirs to be forgotten quickly, and to sink without a ripple the week after its launching.

There are several excellent books by painters which I have read. One by Robert Henri called, I believe, "The Art Spirit." Also, "The Letters of John Constable," and the journal of Eugene Delacroix.

I certainly would much like you as agent for my book if you are willing to wait for the chick to hatch. Unfortunately for me the act of writing is a slow and (unlike painting) a painful one. I have written very little for publication, the most recent an article on the Southwest as seen by a painter which came out in *House and Garden.* (They commissioned me at Tom Lea's generous suggestion since he was unable to accept the offer). It was in the December issue 1954, and if you like I will send you a copy.

As a member of the National Fine Arts Commission I attend the meetings in Washington every month. Usually I stop overnight with our son Peter Wyeth Hurd on the faculty of SMU in the music department.

Thank you for all your kindness, Evelyn. Let's meet when I come and talk over the book idea, and if anything brings you this direction, do come to see us here again *a esta tu casa.*
Peter
Henriette joins me in best wishes.

On February 4, 1961, he wrote:

> Thanks for your warm and gracious note. I began collecting data and ideas for the book and hope to get your ideas when I go through Dallas on the 19th en route to Washington to do a portrait of Barry Goldwater for Time, Inc. I'll stay as before at the Ramada Inn, so convenient to the airport. See you then I hope.
>
> I'm enclosing contract all signed and sealed. Let's hope for Luck.

Then on November 19, 1961, Peter wrote:

> I am working on research for the mural in Austin.
>
> Notes keep accumulating on the book, but so far no prose purple, pink, or otherwise; but don't give up hope.
>
> New airline schedules fly direct from El Paso to the East with only a few minutes stopover in Dallas, so it has been impossible to visit you as before.
>
> Best regards to you and Billie.

By August 20, 1964, Peter wrote:

> Paul Horgan will be in Ft. Worth on October 21st, and Henriette and I also. Do

come over there at the opening of our exhibit, or better yet, next day when we can catch up on everything, including the phantom biography. I do keep assembling notes—but how can I afford the *time?* You can't know of the expensive crew we have (and are) here at the ranch.

See you in Ft. Worth. Meanwhile, warm wishes to you, Evelyn.

He is referring in this letter to an exhibit of his art at the Amon Carter Museum of Western Art in Fort Worth and also the California Palace of the Legion of Honor in San Francisco. For the Fort Worth event Hurd's old friend from their school days together at New Mexico Military Institute, Paul Horgan, wrote his own word picture *Peter Hurd, A Portrait Sketch From Life,* published by the University of Texas Press in 1965. With it was a picture of Peter painted by Henriette in 1926, when life and love were young and art was their world together.

Who will write his biography? And hers? Both will require much knowledge and even more sensitivity.

৵৽৶

By 1948 I realized that the popular demand for my book reviews should not be limited to store and school and church auditoriums, nor the confines of clubs and homes. The biggest audience for books was to go on the air— Radio.

*Evelyn Oppenheimer with Ralph Gilliland in front of
McMurray's Bookshop, with a sign in the corner of the window
reading "Hear Evelyn Oppenheimer for McMurray's KIXL-
1040" (From the collection of the Texas/Dallas History and
Archive Division, Dallas Public Library)*

The president of the Skillern chain of drugstores
agreed with me, and with that sponsor I began broadcasting once a week at night on KRLD Radio in their studio in
Dallas, located in 1948 in the Adolphus Hotel building.
Response came in from as far westward as New Mexico
and Colorado, and it was the southwest that always held

my greatest interest. I was taking off where Alexander Woollcott had left off in the east. Now books had wings, magic wings across time and space.

Oddly enough, though bookstores were the beneficiaries of the programs, as they happily reported, they were not my early sponsors on radio. Skillern's did not even sell books. They just wanted a program which they knew would be of interest and enjoyed. This was true of other sponsors as varied as Interstate Theaters, the Sammy Restaurants of Carlo Messina, Jeunesse Cosmetic Company, and the Swedish Modern Imports company owned by Mrs. Alice Roberts. She was on the Board of Directors of the Dallas Symphony and Opera and the Santa Fe Opera. I often attended the Santa Fe Opera with her in the summer. For all of those sponsors I also wrote and delivered the opening and closing commercials for the program broadcasts.

Then the McMurray Bookshop became sponsor until it was sold to Ralph Gilliland, who continued as sponsor until selling to Doubleday Bookshops which syndicated the program from Dallas-Fort Worth to radio stations in Houston, Phoenix, Los Angeles and San Francisco. That sponsorship through the 1970s was followed by the Southwestern Booksellers Association and then from 1988 to 1993 the Half Price Bookstores. We called my broadcasts "Book Talk," which freed me to discuss old as well as new books and authors. In 1994 the Voyagers Travel and Bookstore, specialists in travel literature, contracted for the program, and its scope of interest has continued to expand for me and my radio audience.

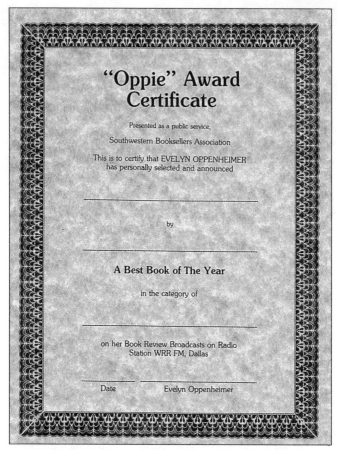

*"Oppie" Award Certificate given by Evelyn Oppenheimer for her
choice of best books of the year in fiction of contemporary and
historical novels and in non-fiction the memoir, biography,
Americana, Texana, humor, current events and history.*

At one time it was suggested that I move from radio to TV, and I did so for about six months. That was more than enough for me when I found myself in a studio with a producer, a director, their respective assistants, and two cameramen. Six people for a one-woman show. I returned to radio as soon as possible to reach again the countless audience in homes, offices, cars, and trucks on all the streets and highways.

Through the more than four decades of my radio book reviewing—a national record—the program moved from KRLD to WFAA to KIXL and then permanently to the municipal station of classical music and arts, WRR FM. There I initiated the award of a certificate called "The Oppie" to my choice of best books of the year. Those awards were in January for the previous year, and included the categories in fiction of contemporary and historical novels and in nonfiction the memoir, biography, Americana, Texana, humor, current events and history.

The certificate of award was sent to the publisher of the books who relayed it to the author. Despite not being monetary nor any kind of elaborate plaque, the awards were received with an appreciation that warmed my heart.

The last of the Oppie Awards was broadcast in January 1987 for the books of 1986. Two went to Margaret George of Wisconsin for her biographical novel tour de force *The Autobiography of Henry VIII* and to Pamela Jekel of California and Maryland for her historical novel of the Pacific Northwest *Columbia*. Both authors wrote letters of appreciation for the Award. Ms. Jekel wrote "I was thrilled and thank you *so* much!" Ms. George wrote "I want to thank you for a very great honor."

Letters of similar warmth had come through the years from Sam Levinson, Louis Nizer, Elizabeth Forsythe Hailey, Louis L'Amour, Walter Lord, Anna Lee Waldo, Tony Hillerman, Irving Stone, Chaim Potok, Arthur Hailey, Harold Kushner, Elizabeth de Trevino, Leon Uris. . . . The list could go on, but the most interesting letter came from Israel dated June 9, 1973.

Its very special interest came from an experience in 1972 that was memorable in many ways. In November of that year St. Martin's Press published the memoir *Champagne Spy* by Israel's most famous espionage agent, Wolfgang Lotz. That true story of what he did in Egypt in the early 1960s out-did any James Bond adventure.

At that time I was also interviewing authors on my book review broadcasts (a practice I later discontinued when it got to be so over-done), and the publicity director at St. Martin's Press wrote me that Lotz would be in Dallas November 20th under the greatest secrecy and they wanted me for his only interview. He was, of course, traveling under an assumed name. We arranged to tape the interview at my home instead of the radio station. Then a close friend and I took him to dinner at one of our finest Italian restaurants, Il Sorrento, after learning that was his favorite cuisine. He asked for a table where his back could be to the wall. All was proceeding well until a dark-skinned waiter came over and spoke to him in Arabic. He had been recognized. We left almost immediately and drove him to the back door of his hotel. What a relief to get him there safely. All the way into downtown Lotz sat in the backseat watching to see if we were being followed. It was a nervous night, to put it mildly.

The interview turned out to be one of the best. Certainly I had never met a more charming, remarkable man. Later the "Champagne Spy" wrote from his home near Tel Aviv:

> Thank you ever so much for the Oppie Award. I consider it a great honour. The certificate now adorns the wall in my study.
>
> Also, let me thank you again for the very pleasant evening in Dallas. There is little chance of my visiting Texas again, but if you ever come this way, please give us the pleasure of visiting us.
>
> Yours sincerely
> Rusty (Lotz's nickname)

The release of Wolfgang Lotz and his wife from prison in Egypt had come only after the Israeli victory in the Six Day War in 1967 when the Israelis told Egypt that only after their release would Israel return some 5000 Egyptian P.O.W.s, including nine generals. Such was the value and importance of him and his work. Long out of print, that book is worth every effort to find and read. Lotz died May 13, 1993, from the one enemy he could not handle, an ailing heart. He was only seventy-three.

Writers, for the most part, and especially the really good ones who have not forgotten their struggle to get publication and success, are appreciative folks. Notable is the fact that the authors of national prominence and distinction have been more ready to express their gratitude for any laudatory recognition than, with a few exceptions, regional or local writers who seem to expect praise and resent any lack of it.

Personally, I have always so enjoyed hearing from an author who takes time to write me. I cherish that as much as some of the awards which have come to me, perhaps most of all one from the Book Publishers of Texas for, to quote from the plaque of bronze and polished wood, "Outstanding Reviewing of Texas Books."

Rereading the letters in my collection at the Bridwell Library evokes memories of those writers and their books. Early in my reviewing career came a letter from Marcia Davenport, daughter of famous operatic and concert singer Alma Gluck and violinist Efrem Zimbalist, who wrote from the 1930s into the 1960s, including a fine biography of Mozart and equally fine novels such as *Of Lena Geyer, The Valley of Decision, My Brother's Keeper*, and *Eastside Westside*. In her letter dated February 19, 1937, she wrote: "I am delighted at your selection of *Lena Geyer* for reviewing and so very glad that you think so highly of the book. The character is fictitious but a composite from the lives of ten of the greatest opera singers who ever lived. Thank you so very much."

One of the first top quality writers in Texas I came to know personally so well was Loula Grace Erdman of West

Texas State College in Canyon, now West Texas A&M University. After my radio review of her Dodd Mead novel *Years of the Locust*, which won the Redbook Award, she wrote on October 9, 1947: "Thanks, Evelyn Oppenheimer. There are times when someone says things in a better way than one would ever think anybody would say them. This you did. I was deeply moved and humbly grateful."

Her novel of the 1950s, *The Edge of Time,* was included in *Classics of Texas Fiction* by Dr. James Ward Lee of the University of North Texas, which I was so glad to see done.

Lillian Hellman wrote a note of appreciation in 1974 for her "Oppie Award Certificate" for her 1973 book *Pentinento.* Ken Follett wrote on February 12, 1984, that he was "delighted and honoured to receive an 'Oppie' for *On Wings of Eagles.* It stands in a frame on the wall of my library, next to the 'Edgar' I won for *Eye of the Needle.* Many thanks indeed!"

Inscribed in one of his books, C. W. Smith graciously wrote "To Evelyn O who kept alive the flame of culture all these years in Dallas. No small task, and an important one!" From Walter Lord, author of *A Time To Stand*, came a letter dated November 18, 1961, in which he wrote, "The interview we did together is the best I have ever had, certainly due to your penetrating approach." (I have a delightful memory of Walter Lord smuggling me into the Princeton Club in New York for lunch one day, where they did not relish serving ladies.)

General W. C. Westmoreland wrote on April 14, 1976, "It was a pleasure to be interviewed by a real 'pro' for a change." The interview he referred to concerned his book *A Soldier Reports,* published by Doubleday in 1976. A letter from Willie Morris dated November 16, 1967, concerning his book *North Toward Home* published by Houghton-Mifflin that same year, included the gracious compliment, "My warmest gratitude for your intelligent, perceptive interview."

I had much correspondence with Irving Stone over the years, including the following excerpt from his letter of January 2, 1986: "What a marvelous review you write. You capture the very essence of a book. The great Dallas area has been fortunate all these years to have your good taste and literary critic skill. . . ." From Sam Levenson, dated January 27, 1967, came this note after the publication of his delightful book *Everything But Money,* published by Simon & Schuster: "I am indeed so proud that you selected me for your Oppie Award in the field of Humor. For my funny book this is a serious honor."

William Barrett, the Denver, Colorado novelist whom I came to know well, wrote in November of 1958:

> Thank you for one of the finest reviews I ever had on any book of mine. Your synopsis of *The Empty Shrine* was a work of art. The average newspaper review either distorts or tells so much of the story that there is no inducement to buy or read. You brought out the people of the story and then stepped aside to let the book take them the rest of the way. That is not easy to do. . . .

And in June of 1963:

> You may have heard that my *Lilies of the Field*
> has been filmed with Sidney Poitier in the lead,
> and it has received the only invitation given a
> US film to the Berlin Film Festival. It is a low
> budget film designated for art houses, but
> Poitier gives the performance of his life, and so
> we may have something. Lilia Skala, a Viennese
> actress who plays the Mother Superior, is re-
> markably good. Thank you again and again for
> all you have done for my books.

He also wrote on May 13, 1975: "Your review script came
in today from Doubleday, and I am delighted with it.
Reaching the big audience that you do—an audience who
tune you in for the prime purpose of learning about books—
the program is bound to awaken interest in my *Lady of the
Lotus.*"

I enjoyed a delightful correspondence with Jean
Gould, after first receiving a letter about her biography of
Edna St. Vincent Millay. In January of 1970 she wrote:

> My publisher, Dodd Mead Co., just sent me the
> certificate announcing that my book *The Poet
> and Her Book* has won the Oppie Award, and I
> want to tell you how very pleased I am!
>
> I have more mail about it than for any of
> my other biographies, including the Robert

Frost. You will be interested to know that one of
my earliest letters came from Edmund Wilson
commending the book for its new material and
general accuracy, concluding with a comment
that I had "At last provided a real biography of
Edna Millay." So you see you have the *other*
Dean of critics in corroboration with you.
In sincere appreciation

In later years she wrote me of her book's selection for
awards from Ohio State University's Ohioana Library
Association and the Bibliotheque Royal de Belgique in
Brussels. We never met, but our minds did.

I had known Frances Sanger Mossiker all my life,
although she was older and made her formal debut at the
Columbian Club—the last debutante event in Dallas Jewish
society at the club—while I was still in high school. With
Fannie was her cousin Phyllis Sanger Pike, whose father
was a partner in the jewelry store Pike & Kramer. Both girls
had all the "flapper" good looks and esprit of the 1920s.

At that time her later international literary eminence
could in no way be foreseen. The daughter of Mr. and Mrs.
Elihu Sanger and grand-daughter of Alex Sanger, with
their homes on South Ervay and Canton streets respec-
tively, her original name was Fannie Alexander Sanger.
Her mother, Evelyn Sanger, was a close friend of my
mother, who named me for her.

A brilliant student at Smith College, Barnard College
and the Sorbonne, Frances' special interest and expertise

was in the French language, history and literature. After an elopement with Frank Beaston of New York in 1925 and divorce in 1932, she returned home and married Dallas merchant Jacob Mossiker, who stabilized her life and encouraged her entry into the book world as a reviewer for *The Dallas Morning News*.

Two decades later, after seven years' research into her favorite subject, eighteenth-century France, the fifty-five year old Dallasite had her first book published, *The Queen's Necklace*. The impact of her version of the famous scandal in the court of Louis XVI was immediate. It became a 1961 bestseller in this country and abroad. After that came her *Napoleon and Josephine* in 1965, *The Affair of the Poisons* in 1969, *Pocahontas–The Life & Legend* in 1976, and her final book in 1983, *Madame de Sevigne, A Life & Letters*. She also wrote one book for young adults entitled *More Than A Queen*, the story of Josephine Bonaparte. Frances died in 1985. Knopf was always her publisher and Robert Gottlieb her editor—an excellent triumvirate.

I was asked by the *Dallas Times Herald* books editor, Jeff Unger, to review *Madame de Sevigne* for their Sunday, January 8, 1984 issue. I wrote:

> *Madame de Sevigne, A Life and Letters* by Frances Mossiker, 538 p. Knopf, $22.95.

> The Texas writer who has gone farthest afield from our borders is Frances Mossiker of Dallas. With one exception, her *Pocahontas*, she has

focused her scholarly research and literary and translation skills on France when Versailles was the center of the so-called civilized world. In fact, even in *Pocahontas* the life story told was of no Comanche, Cherokee, Apache, none of the Southwest Indian world, but of the Northeast.

Mrs. Mossiker's vision of recall is eastern, but that is only a small part of her distinction. Most distinctive are her style and technique as again are so very well presented in her latest book *Madame de Sevigne*. The technique is to combine original documents (letters, in this case) in selected excerpt form interwoven with on-going biographical narrative so that a more authentic, realistic word picture of the person is achieved in a way that restores that person to life. The subject of the biography is not just being written about, but is speaking and present once again. "Live" as they say on radio and TV.

Lively indeed was Madame de Sevigne, a 17th century "Woman of Independent Means" in every sense, a woman whom many American readers get their first real chance to meet and come to know and enjoy in this book.

From her birth in the winter of 1626 to her death in the spring of 1696, Marie de Rabutin-Chantal, the Marquise de Sevigne, lived a life that fulfilled her every potential of intellect and personality. Charm and beauty and the gentility of aristocratic background were bonus assets to a strength of character put to test by her husband's abuse and scandalous behavior. When he was killed in a duel over an affair with another woman, she was free and only twenty-five years old. Her life was before her, and she kept it that way. No more marriages, despite multiple proposals. Society was her interest and the observation of people her talent. She should have been a novelist.

Instead she was to become famous for her one weakness, her idolatry of her daughter. In her daily, almost hourly letters when they were apart, she not only poured out her excessive love and devotion but, and more important, the news of the day with her commentary. There was a son too, but he was forever secondary or less in her heart, a situation he accepted with remarkable grace.

However, when mother and daughter were together, there was more tension than rapport. Letters can be cathartic and relieve and satisfy the writer, whereas personal confrontation can be frustrating. In Madame's era so long before the AT&T slogan, she knew how to "reach out and touch someone" not just for minutes but for centuries. With her pen.

The book deserves a top award.

Frances responded in a letter of January 11, 1984:

> Whatever the protocol regarding the priority of a writer's response to a review of her oeuvre, I am acting on impulse in writing to tell you that I was pleased as punch at the review you did of *Mme De Sevigne* for the *Times Herald* last Sunday.
>
> I value your good opinion and graceful expression of it as a splendid example of the reviewer's craft.
>
> I now have Madame to thank for having our paths cross again—yours and mine—after too long an estrangement.
>
> I'm still slaving away at the French edition. As soon as I have accomplished that, I'll call for a dinner date.
>
> A happy 1984!
>
> Fondly,
> Frances

The estrangement she referred to in that letter had been caused by one of her friends in the local literary sanctuary. We took care of that matter at a delightful dinner together.

New York and Boston publishers were in steady contact with me as their sales flourished in areas they knew little if anything about—the southwest. Few of their editors had ever ventured west of the Hudson River, much less the

Mississippi. Notable exceptions of course were Alfred and Blanche Knopf, who made several trips to Texas where I had the pleasure of visiting with them. They were a couple of majestic dignity. It was hard to tell who was the stronger in the unique partnership of literary vision and love of Americana which they shared.

For a number of years I made an annual pilgrimage to the shrine of the eastern publishers. Once I was referred to in New York as "a literary catalyst," which I appreciated as a compliment until discovering some confusion at that martini luncheon table about the word catalyst and owning cattle. Regrettably, I have never even owned a calf.

I no longer make that pilgrimage. With so many of the major eastern publishers having become cogs in the big wheels of corporate conglomerates, the result is only a narrowing of interest down to instant microwave commercialism, instead of any literary quality. In my judgment, the potential of publishing has moved westward at last to small publishers and expanding university presses, not only for new books and new writers but for reprints of books of value which have gone out of print.

Such publishers in the southwest, northwest and midwest still have some editors who know how and when to edit, especially to delete, no matter the fame of the author's name. Every word is not as sacred as some writers think.

3

Branching Out

On one of my rather regular trips to Lubbock for a book review program, sponsored by the Lubbock National Bank at that time, my friend and a vice-president of the bank who hosted those affairs, Ruth Ford, spoke of the great need to inform women, especially older women, about their financial affairs. Was there a way to do this so that it could be entertaining as well as educational? She was keenly aware that in the 1960s and 1970s there was a generation of women, many of them widows, who had never been taught anything by their husbands or fathers about such matters.

I came up with the idea for a series to be called "Finance Fashioned For Women." We began with a program on wills, a subject which she and I considered most vital, even when there is no family.

That opening program was very successful and drew a big audience. I pointed out the need to list and provide for all their material possessions in the future—how, where, and to whom they wished those possessions to go. I stressed too the necessity to review a will at regular intervals because time brings many changes in our relationships. It could kill us again if we knew that the diamond ring we planned to go to brother Bill ended up on a finger of his new wife whom we simply can't stand. And what about our cut glass and our Limoges china? Surely not to cousin Jane after the way she has been acting lately. And our books— those first editions of Hemingway—where will they be really safe and properly valued? Or that original Cortez rainswept Paris scene?

The ladies began to see that there is more to think about than stocks and bonds, CDs, land and real estate. There are also the deeply personal treasures which we inherit and collect through a lifetime. Word got around about the success of those programs in Lubbock, and the Texas Bank and Trust in Dallas engaged me to present several of them to an invited audience.

It was not long before I could and did make a connection between those lectures and the novels emerging about women in the business world, such as Barbara Bradford's *Woman of Substance* and its sequels.

Meanwhile, I was getting more and more inquiries from many persons, mostly women but some men too, about where they could learn about this new profession of oral book reviewing. No college or university offered such a course, and there was no textbook on the subject. Ergo, I wrote *Book Reviewing for an Audience, A Practical Guide in Techniques for Lecture and Broadcast,* published by the Chilton Company in Philadelphia in 1962. Five reprints followed that first edition. Dr. DeWitt Reddick, Director of the School of Journalism at the University of Texas at Austin at that time, contributed the introduction. The jacket cover included this quote from novelist Irving Stone, "The oral review is a special art form. At this art form Evelyn Oppenheimer is a master. She is able to review a book orally in such a way that a whole community begins to read it at once. This is a valuable and masterly service!" In 1980, the book was published in a revised edition by Scarecrow Press of the Grolier Company under the title *Oral Book Reviewing to Stimulate Reading.*

In it I included a section of sample reviews of various lengths and genres, the reviews written from previous notes. I believe in having notes in order to keep organized, for timing, and for any emergency mental lapse about dates or names. The reviews I included were of *Gone With the Wind, Ethan Frome, The Glass Menagerie, The Rise and Fall of the Third Reich, The Agony and Ecstacy, The Old Man and the Sea, The Nazarene* (two versions for different timing), *Hound-Dog Man, The King and I, Roots, The Patton Papers, Agatha Christie, Sacajawea, My Name Is Asher Lev,* and *The Origin.* The range in years was from 1936 to 1980, five decades.

Academic awareness of the need to supply the demand for a course of instruction in this new profession began in west Texas when I was asked to teach an intensive course on the subject at Amarillo College. Then in 1957 I was asked to teach the course at Texas Tech University in Lubbock. In the summer of 1958 the University of Texas at Austin engaged me to present the course there, and in 1960 I was asked to repeat it.

The University of California in Los Angeles also had me teach the course there in 1958. The University of Dallas requested it in 1959. Then Southern Methodist University in Dallas had me give the course in the School of Continuing Education in 1970, and its success generated a repeat. A request then came from the University of Wisconsin to condense the course for a lecture which I gave by phone hook-up to their extension department.

I thoroughly enjoyed that teaching and getting to know the women and men in all those classes. They were people who cared, really cared, about books—good books—in whatever genre. I recall that many of the people in these classes were librarians who were being called upon to review books for special programs. We all shared our knowledge and love of books in exciting discussions and wonderful times together.

I confess a great fondness for librarians. They are the quiet custodians of our most valuable treasure. They need to be less quiet. They need to call much more attention to themselves for what they can guide you to and what they guard. I have long contended that a public library card is the best credit card that can be given to any child or adult. Most regretfully I have had to watch my city show more concern for supporting sports arenas than the public library and its growing need for books, services, equipment. A city can be judged by its public library.

Prior to my book on reviewing, publisher Joe Naylor of San Antonio, Texas, who knew of my induction into the Chicago Poetry Society, had been in contact for a collection of the poems which had qualified me for that membership. In 1951 he published my book *Legend and Other Poems*. The title narrative poem came from an old legendary romance I had heard about at the Villa d'Este on Lake Como during my first trip to Italy. It was redolent of moonlight and Chianti, but the other poems ranged from lyric to satiric, and I am still not ashamed of them. Poetry is always the beginning, the first and most natural sound of thought. From that we either ascend or descend into prose, however you choose to put it. But if the prose is good, the echo of the poet is always in it.

A sampling from that little book of sixty-two pages is included in "Lagniappe" on page 140 of this book.

Early in the 1960s the retired District Clerk of Red River County, Mr. Eugene W. Bowers of Clarksville, got in touch with me concerning his collection of the most interesting historical records of what had been a frontier settlement and town before any others in the nineteenth century in north and northeast Texas.

Mr. Bowers' father had preceded him as District Clerk from 1878 to 1890, and so their combined court records, diaries and letters held invaluable human interest stories of drama and comedy for popular appeal, whereas just the collection itself would only gather dust on an academic shelf. Accordingly an agreement was made so that I would select the material and write it in narrative form as a book of documented true stories, and we would be collaborators. I was able to get the late and great historian and columnist Frank X. Tolbert of *The Dallas Morning News* to write the introduction. He led off with the following: "I was surprised when I heard that these two had teamed together for a book—Eugene Bowers, in my opinion Texas' most diligent cracker-barrel historian, and Evelyn Oppenheimer, one of the nation's most respected literary authorities, an intellectual and author of the bible on book reviewing."

I titled the book *Red River Dust* and it was first published by Word Books of Waco in 1968. It went into several printings, and then in 1980 a new edition was published by Eakin Press of Austin. William A. Owens of Columbia University, who was born in Pin Hook in the Clarksville area, wrote to applaud the book, "Dust in the title—Life in the pages!"

In 1970 Mr. Walter Frese, president of Hastings House Publishing Company in New York, asked me to prepare a book on Texas for their *Profiles of America* series. After a year's intensive work, *Texas In Color* was published in 1971 and continued in many reprints. There are thirty-two full color illustrations, most of which I selected from pictures from the Texas Highway Department. Four came from private photographers. One of those pictures, that of Kilgore with its streets cluttered with oil derricks, is now a collector's item, as the streets have long since been cleared.

Another picture, an aerial view of the South Texas citrus valley, had an odd special interest, as it was alleged to have held a secret directive for the military in case of Japanese attack on this continent in the Second World War. I was never able to substantiate that intriguing tidbit.

Early in the 1960s Droke House Publishing Company of Anderson, South Carolina, had also contacted me about

Evelyn signing Red River Dust *at House of Books in 1983.*

writing a book on public speaking for women. Certainly there was need for it with more and more women on the lecture platform, into politics and all forms of civic work. I was aware too that the woman speaker faces certain challenges which are distinctive and can present some problems.

I got in touch with actress Ilka Chase whose weekly national radio program "Luncheon at the Waldorf" was such a popular delight, and she agreed to write the Introduction. In it she said: "The Oppenheimer book is a genuine help to women all over America who are speaking publicly more and more. . . . Her tips are so specific, wise, sound, effective."

The book was published in 1968 under the title *The Articulate Woman*. Later in 1976 the Pyramid Company of New York, a division then of Harcourt, Brace, Jovanovich, published it in a revised mass paperback edition. An updated edition of that book is certainly indicated now with the proliferation of women as speakers. That project is on my schedule for the very near future. Few women in the clergy, the business and professional worlds, and on radio and television speak as well as they should and could, too few.

Then in 1975 the New York agent and former salesman for Doubleday in Texas, Aaron Priest, came to me and to Bill Porterfield, who was then with the PBS television station Channel 13 in Dallas, and told us that Doubleday Publishing Company wanted a book about Dallas with us as co-editors. It would be a deluxe book with texts by local luminaries. These leaders would write on the history of the various parts of metropolitan life in which each was an expert and an outstanding success. Doubleday had previously published with much success such coffee-table size books on several other cities.

We were to cover the topics of banking, industry, mercantile retailing, religion, politics, sports, real estate, education, arts. I would have preferred including the field

Evelyn sitting at her desk working on Book of Dallas.

of medical developments instead of politics, but I was out-voted on that. In addition, we hoped we would get a special introduction from former mayor and philanthropist, Erik Jonsson. Because of personal contacts I was to make the arrangements with the persons selected as writers. Each of the writers was to receive an honorarium of a thousand dollars from Doubleday, which several donated to charity.

The writers were Erik Jonsson for the Introduction; Walter J. Humann on Industry; Stanley Marcus on Mercantile Life; Raymond D. Nasher on Real Estate; W. W. Overton, Jr., of Texas Bank and Trust on Finance; Blackie Sherrod then of the *Dallas Times Herald* and now of *The Dallas Morning News* on Sports; Dr. Bill J. Priest, then Dallas County Community College District Chancellor, on Education; Toni Beck, the dancer, choreographer and head of the Dance Department at Southern Methodist University, covered The Arts—Fine and Performing.

My first choice for the section on Religion was the great scholar Dr. Albert Outler of Perkins School of Theology at Southern Methodist University, but because of another publishing commitment for his work on John Wesley, he instead recommended Dr. Levi Olan, Rabbi Emeritus of Temple Emanu-El of Dallas, who agreed to write it and did an outstanding history and analysis.

Bill Porterfield arranged with A. C. Greene for the chapter on Politics and then with prize-winning photographers Laura Garza and Bob Smith for 180 photographs in color and 128 photographs in black and white.

Porterfield and I each wrote Prefaces and Epilogues.

After months of the most diligent work on the book, during which time I maintained my radio reviewing schedule and taught various facets of modern literature at the Southern Methodist University School of Continuing Education, the completed manuscript with illustrations and design for the *Book of Dallas* were personally delivered to Doubleday by Porterfield in the winter of 1976. Advance promotion and sales were very big. Books were to be ready for shipment in October or early November for the holiday season. The book was priced at $35.00, with a limited edition signed, numbered and leather-bound at $150.00 (no copy of which I ever saw).

Then the misery began. The agent and the Doubleday editors had become embroiled in a hostile relationship. The printing company was stricken with some sort of paralysis. Everybody connected with the project in New York blamed everybody else. There were no books ready to fill the orders. Finally a few dozen were flown into Dallas where some bookstore managers met the plane a couple of weeks before Christmas. All autograph parties had to be canceled except a small suburban one. It was a severe professional shock to me. I became ill from all the trauma and suffered a severe nasal hemorrhage, and had to spend the holiday season in the hospital. Then one of the photographer-artists was killed in a plane crash.

Such was the saga of disaster for a unique and invaluable book, for not before or since has there been one at all comparable in combining so many talents on a metropolitan subject. Not until January 1977 were copies ready to be shipped, and by then the publisher's regional sales representative was unequal to the job of handling the situation. Thus, the comedy of errors continued as the book was finally remaindered to lucky buyers who now own a collectors item.

A reprint of just the text would certainly be of much historic interest and value, especially in view of the fact that on April 16, 1977, the Geographic Society of Chicago gave *The Book of Dallas* its prestigious Publication Award for 1976, with the following words of acclaim:

> *The Book of Dallas* adds to the literature on metropolitan areas. The development of Dallas is told through words and pictures by the men and women who helped in the making of a diversified area shifting from agriculture to industry and professions transforming a frontier town to a modern sophisticated city which has stood for both East and West in a special combination. It shows Texas independence and an open, easy-going way of life with development on a grand scale by its own rules. More than any other city of the Southwest, it is founded on a long tradition of big business, wealth and a glitter of social life, culture, elegance, and high fashion. It is the vitality of this mixture which keeps Dallas in a class by itself. This book is a portrait of man's endeavors and hopes for tomorrow.

No other book on Dallas ever received such national recognition and award.

For recovery that summer, I went with my friend Billie Billingsley and her nine pound fox terrier to the western Colorado wilderness where Rocky Mountain altitude never fails to restore perspective. There, on a good horse, where the rivers are home to trout and beaver, where the marmots whistle on the boulders and where deer and elk are belly-high in grass and columbine—there was and is healing.

Back in the man-made world of books the sick psyche of the 1960s was pervading the 1970s, even though a few quality writers such as Irving Stone, Herman Wouk, Chaim Potok, Leon Uris, and the early Michener were creating and producing against the trend of sex and horror and crime, all under the Freudian umbrella. The couch and the bed were operating on an alternating current. The word decadence was too un-American to apply. It lay buried in the dictionary or among the ruins of the Roman Empire.

Only one writer, a woman who was so honest that she made no claim to being a writer, gave us a bestseller of major importance—the first exposé of the use of drugs in our society's biggest entertainment industry—*Valley of the Dolls*. The author of that non-literary bombshell and eye-opener on Hollywood was Jacqueline Susann, a lady I came to know and highly respect.

As a member of the advisory committee of the Wellesley College Benefit Book and Author Luncheon, an annual event of established success in Dallas, I urged the program committee to invite Jacqueline Susann for their 1966 affair. After much hesitation they agreed. A standing-room-only audience filled the old Sheraton Hotel ballroom auditorium, all of them expecting to be shocked by a Hollywood tramp. Instead the shock was the sight of a handsome, gracious woman, perfect in manner, speech and dress. With her was her husband of equal charm and sophistication. Dallas was impressed, and, more important, heard a message of serious warning which, alas, proved all too true.

Pierre Salinger was also on that program, but who cared?

I was helpful too in getting novelist William Barrett (*Lilies of the Field, Left Hand of God*, and others) in 1968, William Morris of the American Heritage Dictionary in 1969, New York publisher-editor Sam Vaughn in 1970, and in 1980 biographical novelist Irving Stone and his wife and editor Jean, to come as stellar speakers for the Wellesley Benefits. The Stones had become my very dear friends. Since his death in 1989 I keep waiting for the fine biography which his career deserves.

In 1977 a group of us under the leadership of premier bookman Marvin Steakley organized the Southwestern Booksellers Association. Members included publisher sales representatives, librarians, reviewers, agents, and publishers, as well as bookstore personnel. The group presented a Book and Author Dinner at the Fairmount Hotel that was memorable. In addition to Tommy Thompson, author of the bestseller on the sensational Joan Robinson murder case in Houston, *Blood and Money*, I was instrumental in getting my friend Elithe Hamilton Kirkland, Texas' best historical novelist, and the one and only Louis L'Amour, whose brilliant lecture on American frontier literature I have never heard equaled. With him was his handsome wife, and the audience and speakers all had a fine time together as books sales kept the cash registers ringing like Poe's "tintinnabulation of the bells, bells, bells. . . ." Another huge success was rung up by the Southwestern Booksellers when we brought James Clavell at the peak of his *Shogun* popularity. As a speaker, however, he was better off in the Orient.

Many authors of distinction have come to Dallas to promote their books, and I interviewed many of them on my radio program until I stopped that practice. Few writers are good speakers or have much to say beyond what they have written. Some are egotistical bores. Top bore was Florida doctor-novelist Frank Slaughter whose multiple bestsellers and M.D. degree had gone to his head and severely enlarged his ego.

But there have been many wonderful men and women and personal contact with them has been an enriching experience for me. Best of all, I remember the visit with the great William Shirer, a quiet man, comfortable to be with, as the truly big persons always are.

The most delightful interview I recall was with opera star Renata Scotto about her book of memoirs *More than a Diva*, published by Doubleday in 1984. She was charming, utterly unpretentious, honest and generated a warmth with a wonderful sense of humor—seldom the traits of a prima donna. Whenever I see a production of *Madama Butterfly*, I can hear only the perfection of Scotto's Cio-Cio-San.

A very special memory is of a dinner with Agatha Christie who came to Dallas incognito (she thought) accompanying her husband Sir Max Mallowan on his lecture tour for various archaeology societies. I had the pleasure of sitting next to Dame Christie that evening. Her main concern was that she had to wear old tennis shoes with her floor length dinner dress because her feet hurt so badly. I assured her that not even Hercule Poirot would suspect her secret if we were the last to leave the table, and then slipped out the club's kitchen door. It worked!

Stephen Birmingham, who wrote so well of *Our Crowd* and its multiple variations, was a charmer. But the author who sold more of his own excellent books than anyone I ever knew was that historian of New Orleans and the bayous and *Deep Delta Country* and Natchez and the Old South—Harnett Kane. We had delightful visits in Dallas and New Orleans, and once, by sheer chance, in London, where we happened to meet at the theatre and then survived fish and chips in Soho.

The parade of authors continues today as they try to compete with other performers in order to do what their publishers fail to do—sell books. Most of them are not very good at it. Television has made celebrity a cheap commodity.

The decade of the 1970s brought several very fine books of enduring value, one of which—Alex Haley's

Roots—was to have the most major impact on our sociology of any book of the century. Others such as Wouk's *Winds of War* and *War and Remembrance* and Uris's *QB7* and *Exodus* documented the horrors of the holocaust forever.

Except for writers such as Barbara Tuchman, Doris Kearns Goodwin, and Dee Brown (*Bury My Heart at Wounded Knee*), even nonfiction had succumbed to the trend in sex and self-help. The next decade of the 1980s was to improve very little as biography seemed to drown in the Potomac and Pedernales with LBJ.

However, what applied on the so-called literary scene (as defined by the east) was fortunately not true in some other regions. Certainly Texas writers had something valid to say about the past and the present, and for some time had been and were writing it on high quality level. There were authors such as Benjamin Capps, Elmer Kelton, John Graves, Tom Lea, Al Dewlen, J. Evetts Haley, Fred Gipson, Jane Gilmore Rushing, Curry Holden, Leonard Sanders, Robert Flynn, Ramon Adams, Clay Reynolds, Jane Roberts Wood, Elizabeth Hailey, Richard Haddaway, David Fleming. . . .

Here I am interjecting a commentary which is in no way a digression. On the contrary, it is a closely related observation about the book world in America that has festered within me through recent years. I think of it as "the case of the western transplant."

The protagonist is the eastern critics' habit of looking down their nostrils at the western short story or novel as "the shoot-em-up," the implication being that this was the lowest rung on the literary ladder. That stance was taken toward writers whose narrative expertise with authentic history was seldom even known, except for Willa Cather and Mari Sandoz. But of A. B. Guthrie, Jr., Frank Waters, David Lavender, Jack Schaeffer and their peers, little was known or valued in the province of Manhattan. There they never seemed to realize that all literature is regional—the setting of the contents of a book—whether it be east, west, south or north. That is simply how books reflect geography. Nothing has been more regional than the novels by Louis Auchincloss and John Marquand, but critics never noted that disparagingly, nor with Faulkner or Welty. Only the West gets judged as something separate and apart for reasons of inexplicable prejudice or ignorance (or envy?). What is regional in setting has no effect on being universal in content.

So far, too, those critics fail to see that the same patterns of human behavior considered limited to the West are being written about today in the bestsellers of crime violence in the suspense category. Only the settings have changed from rural frontier to urban society everywhere. The guns are more sophisticated. The ambushes in box canyons have become electronic bugging. The old shipments of gold and silver are now drugs. The saloon ladies are elevated to espionage sex bait. In brief, the shoot-em-ups have moved eastward and into hi-tech in the good vs. evil confrontation, and their critics are unaware of the trick that time has played upon them.

I presented much of the fertility of our literary landscape in the series of lectures I gave in the School of

Continuing Education at Southern Methodist University in
the 1980s. One course was on books that influenced our
lives, and there were more of them than one might think,
until we really *do* think about the effect of those from Tom
Paine and Harriet Beecher Stowe to Rachel Carson, Nevil
Shute, Freud, Hitler, Anne Frank, Alex Haley, George
Orwell and Aldus Huxley, for example.

In one summer's session I took a class on a detour I
called "Shakespeare Once Over Spritely," a title facetious
enough to be attractive. I gave them a new look at the
master as the first great psychologist three hundred long
years before Freud was to put that word into popular
currency and on academic curricula. The course really
grew out of a series of radio programs I had broadcast in
1953 and 1954 which were sponsored by Interstate Theatres and two very popular Dallas restaurants at that time,
Sammy's and Town and Country. The success of that radio
series, as proved by public response, showed me how
eager people of all ages were to be introduced to Shakespeare
in a way that showed them how timeless his plays are in
relating to human characters and situations.

We recognize many persons we know in the senseless
and often tragic feuding of families in *Romeo and Juliet*, the
grief and indecision, disillusionment and commitment to
avenge a wrong in *Hamlet*, the problem of old age—which
today we call geriatrics—in *Lear*, the cost of guilt from evil
in *Macbeth*, for example. Once pointed out, we relate to
such things, and Elizabethan language is no longer a
barrier but an adornment, a sort of ornamental frame. "To

be or not to be" is simply another way of saying, "To live
or not to live," perhaps even a better way.

The same satisfaction came in another course I called
"Books to Remember." It was a joy to guide those men and
women to books which most of them had missed, books
such as the brilliant satire of Edgar Lee Masters's *Spoon
River Anthology,* with its collection of tombstone epitaphs in
a cemetery telling the real truth about the folks buried
there, or the exquisite romance of Richard Aldington's
narrative poem, "A Dream in the Luxembourg," published in England in 1930 and later in New York in 1946 by
Covici under the title "Love and the Luxembourg." Previously he had written the great World War I novel *Death of
a Hero*, a match any day for Ernest Hemingway's *Farewell
to Arms*. They knew Kahlil Gibran's *The Prophet* and some
knew *The Rubaiyat* but not the *Kasidah*. Too few knew the
great American novels of Wallace Stegner or the Romain
Rolland French masterpiece *Jean Christophe,* which I
reread at least every other year to restore me.

I found that many in my classes and audiences had
never heard of or read the delicious humor of Don Marquis
in *Archy and Mehitabel*, the essays and poems of E. B.
White, the great narrative poem "Tristram" by Edwin
Arlington Robinson, the short stories of Katherine Mansfield
and those of "Saki" by H. H. Munro. A few knew of Oscar
Wilde, mainly because of the homosexuality case, but
there was woeful ignorance of his great essays, novels,
plays, poetry.

I found too that most of those university graduates
knew little or nothing about Anatole France, John Gals-

worthy, Voltaire, Joseph Conrad, Somerset Maugham's short stories (except for "Rain"), or James Branch Cabell whose novel *Jurgen* was suppressed in 1919. It was an eye-opening exposure on the limitations of their so-called college education. These people simply had the barest background in literature, and they were readers looking for guidance.

Least of all was their knowledge of Texas and other western writers. Most of them were unaware of the high quality that evolved in the books of Louis L'Amour, master of frontier history and psyche, novels such as *The Sacketts, Lonesome Gods, The Haunted Mesa, Last of the Breed*, and his memoir of self-education as a reader and book collector, *Education of a Wandering Man.*

They kept up with Frank Tolbert's popular column in *The Dallas Morning News* on the history, geography and sociology of Texas, but only a few knew of his books, as authentic as they were maverick in style. They only knew of his classic on the cooking of his famous chili, *A Bowl of Red*, with its delightful detours into allied subjects such as S.O.B. Stew, a concoction almost as dear to the real cowboy as his horse.

Tolbert and his family and I had long been friends, and it was a sad day for me on January 10, 1984, when I was told that he had died in his sleep the night before. That spring I went to work on a biography of the man who had plowed his own fertile field of Texana and always turned his back on the politics of his peers and the prizes and awards they gave each other. With the complete cooperation of his widow, his daughter Kathleen Ryan and his son Frank X. Tolbert II, I wrote the biography and edited excerpts added from his *Informal History of Texas* ("history with the hair and hide left on"), *The Day of San Jacinto, Dick Dowling at Sabine Pass*, his great historical novel of the Texas and Plains Indians, *The Staked Plain,* and that classic novel of southwestern humor, *Bigamy Jones.* From all the

Evelyn holding Tolbert of Texas *at the book signing at Tolbert's Restaurant in downtown Dallas in 1986.*

vast material of his writing career I selected and included
several of his stories from the *Saturday Evening Post* and
from his book *Neiman-Marcus, Texas*, his *Dallas Morning
News* columns, *A Bowl of Red*, and feature stories as com-
bat correspondent and later editor of the U. S. Marines
publication *Leatherneck* during World War II.

The book was published in 1986 by Texas Christian
University Press in both hard and soft cover, its title *Tolbert
of Texas, The Man and His Work*.

At the book signing for Tolbert of Texas, *Evelyn is flanked
by* Dallas Morning News *columnists Bob St. John (left) and
John Anders*

That same year I had a children's story for Christmas published by Hendrick-Long Company, titled *Tilli Comes to Texas*. The book is the story of a Canadian blue spruce tree, with its Indian name Tilli for Tillicum, brought to Texas for holiday sale. It was a story that had been evolving in my head for a long time. Always I had hated the sight of beautiful Christmas trees thrown out like garbage after the holiday season. Always, too, I have hated the way that people forget and dispense with the holiday spirit of giving as soon as the holidays are over. All the way homeward from British Columbia one summer I began a simple little story that would project those thoughts in a way that anyone of any age could see how human love and the love of nature should never be limited to any one time on the calendar. Then "Tilli" just wrote itself.

కా•ఆ

May I digress for a moment on that memory of the spruce-forested Canadian Rockies? I see them sloping into our American Rockies and recall my many summers in the shadow of the Grand Tetons of Wyoming and the San Juans and West Elk Wilderness of Colorado where books became those by David Lavender and Muriel Wolle. I look at those books now in their well-worn bindings and see again that awesome high country so densely wooded and then snow-capped over the massive bare peaks with boulders jutting out. It puts you in your place, your proper place.

Between the peaks and canyons the little villages and meadows, lush with columbine and lupine where mountain streams run like tiny veins, all wait for me to come again. Forever waiting are the ghost towns, those old skeletal, long-deserted mining shafts on mountain sides and cliffs pock-marked with holes where men dug dreams and dared to die and be forgotten.

From my pages of memory as well as from books comes the smell of forests cool and green and white and gold with aspen. Like the blue spruce, there is distinction in an aspen tree. What is special is not just its beauty, a poetic beauty shaped like a sonnet, but the touch of its gleaming white, cool bark and the almost formal, stately distance that separates the trees so that ferns can grow between them and catch those trembling leaves when they let fall their gold.

Always in riding through such a forest grove, I leaned from my horse to reach out and touch those white trunks and feel their coolness, for even in summer it is there as if the snow had just left them.

There is a new learning to be read as it is written on the earth when one rides the trails in the high country, and the lessons come from simple, quiet men—the local wranglers and guides—who have a knowledge which can humble the sophisticate. To look at the trail before you, which your horse's feet have usually found first, and to learn to see the difference between fresh deer or elk tracks and then confirm that by their round droppings, this becomes an exciting new journey in research apart from any library.

Evelyn leading the parade for The Cattleman's Days Rodeo in Gunnison, Colorado, July 1982. (Photographer C & B Moore Photography. Courtesy Evelyn Oppenheimer)

You of only metropolitan background, do I hear you exclaim in disgust about what possible importance, much less excitement there can be in the sight of animal excrement? I pity you, for then I know that you have never been in the wilderness, never known the places where you feel the long fingers of nature reaching out to hold us as they did with our pioneer fathers and mothers. To recognize animal tracks and droppings is to know that wildlife is near and there is the chance to see the flash of a brown body in all its ballet grace of haste to escape into its own solitude. There and then you stand among your kin.

Nor is such experience so inspiring to writers in any way limited to our high country of Wyoming, Colorado, New Mexico, California and the Northwest. I have responded to it, as others have, just as keenly in the semi-arid high terrain and canyons of the Big Bend and Guadalupe Mountains in West Texas.

The biggest of all books to learn to read is The Earth. The poets have always known this, not only Wordsworth or Shelley or Longfellow, but also Maya Angelou today in "A Rock, A River, A Tree," and the great poem "On the Pulse of Morning," which she read so eloquently at the inauguration of President Bill Clinton, January 20, 1993.

$$\approx\!\infty$$

Simple, elemental, eternal verities of nature surround us. Simplest of all are the words of wisdom from the late scholar Abram J. Herschel: "Two great events happened in the world today effecting all the world. The sun rose, and the sun set."

No one would have appreciated that more than the man whose biography was destined to be my next book, the pioneer horticulturist Gilbert Onderdonk of New York and Texas, but mostly Texas.

It all began to happen one evening in 1989 when a friend, Mrs. Allen (Sally) Butler of Dallas, brought me several boxes of papers which had been stored in various homes of her family in south Texas for four generations. She is the great-granddaughter of the man who wrote those papers. When I began to read them I felt the thrill of a discovery in Texas and American history. Onderdonk's name was not to be found in the history books, except in the records of the U. S. Department of Agriculture. They did not include him because his story was only in those boxes and his letters and other private papers and records which had been so long stored away. I felt like an archaeologist who comes upon a dig of treasures from the past. Immediately I went to work on what would be the book published by the University of North Texas Press in the spring of 1991, *Gilbert Onderdonk, The Nurseryman of Mission Valley, Pioneer Horticulturist*.

It is the story of the man himself, as a person and also as a writer and scientist, which was as fascinating as the national importance of his work in literally planting the fruit growing industry of Texas. All the colorful adventure of the latter half of the nineteenth century comes alive in his letters to his grandfather in New York and his travel reports

on Mexico, the first of their kind by an American. In our
research, my editor Frances Vick and I ran down copies of
Onderdonk's catalogues on all his orchard's produce at
Mission Valley and Nursery, copies we found all the way
from the Barker Texas History Center at the University of
Texas in Austin to the University of Delaware Library
Special Collections at Newark, which dated back to 1870.
In them he gave information as good for the horticulturist
today as then. I fell in love with that frail young Yankee who
came to Texas for his health and learned to rope a wild

*Evelyn with Onderdonk descendants at a signing in Victoria,
May, 1991.*

mustang and court a girl as expertly as he cross-bred a peach or fought as a Confederate soldier.

The book won instant award from the San Antonio Conservation Society, and has been highly recommended by various horticultural journals here and abroad. It was ignored by the state's historical and literary societies as they

Evelyn speaking with Rosemary Rumbley at the signing for Gilbert Onderdonk: The Nurseryman of Mission Valley, Pioneer Horticulturist *in 1991.*

chose to remain unaware of this pioneer of a century ago whose fruit we continue to enjoy from the now famous Rio Grande Valley. New growth takes longer with people than with plants.

Books authored or edited by Evelyn Oppenheimer include: Tolbert of Texas, The Articulate Woman, Heroes of Texas, The Book of Dallas, Texas in Color, Red River Dust, Legend and Other Poems, Tilli Comes to Texas, Oral Book Reviewing to Stimulate Reading *and* Book Reviewing for an Audience.
Not shown is Gilbert Onderdonk.

Here perhaps is as good a time and place as any to inject a word of caution to writers and readers which I have learned from my own research work: Do not believe everything you read. Print in any form does not make it gospel. Writers do not always do enough research, and historians and biographers can be as guilty of this as novelists. Even in writing this memoir I came upon a glaring error made by a publisher and editor of another book in giving the date of a nineteenth-century writer's lecture on literature in England five years *after* the man had died. I also came across a famous author's name spelled entirely differently in a biographical dictionary and in an encyclopedia.

Such things make research an almost endless job, but a fascinating one. Nothing becomes a fact until it is verified as completely as possible. Historians such as Barbara Tuchman and Doris Kearns Goodwin know that, and so do the best, though not always best-seller novelists as diverse as Wallace Stegner and Louis L'Amour. Certainly the sadly declining number of truly professional and dedicated editors know it.

Often I am asked how I do my own writing, as if there were some secret process which one employs. My answer is that I use paper and a pencil with a good eraser. This simple answer seems to deliver a tremendous shock. Surely I can't be that antiquarian.

Yes, I can.

I also use a very old and reliable Royal portable typewriter, manual of course.

Do I have fax and computer equipment? No.

How do I manage without such things? Very well, as did all the writers before our time.

Antiques have their value.

Agent by Accident

One night in 1961 I was in the railroad station in Amarillo after giving a review program and waiting for the train to Fort Worth and Dallas. Seeing me safely off, though safety was not such a problem then, was a young woman I had come to know in my audience and classes there, Margaret Abrams.

She had gone through a divorce, had two children, and she was dedicated to writing. She asked if I would read her manuscript of a novel and act as her agent. I told her that I was not an agent, but she insisted that she wanted someone she knew and trusted and who was considerably closer than New York agents. She pointed out, too, that a number of other Texas writers would feel that way about it since agents were becoming necessary to get a publisher's attention.

I began to think it over and took her manuscript with me. As soon as I read it and I saw how thoroughly professional and excellent it was in style, character study, and charm, I changed one last sentence and sent it to an editor I knew well at Houghton Mifflin. They took it and it was published in 1962 as *The Uncle*, the story of a seven-year-old boy who suddenly finds that he is an uncle to another seven-year-old boy. The consequences affect a family situation. The book was of appeal to every age reader.

The little novel got the most laudatory review by *Kirkus* as "utterly enchanting." The author and I went to New York where I arranged for Robert Lantz to work with me to handle certain subsidiary rights. All went wonderfully well—too well as it turned out. Hodder and Stoughton of London took it for an English edition, and Germany followed with a translation by a Hamburg publisher.

I kept Margaret working on her next novel, *Seasons of the Heart*, and it was published in 1964 by Houghton Mifflin. Then a strange momentum of events began. Play-Pix of England bought rights to *The Uncle* for a movie to be made there with Desmond Davis as director. Margaret went to England as consultant and in the process became, as they say, romantically involved.

I went to New York to see the preview of the finished picture with the Houghton Mifflin editor, Joyce Hartman. The movie was perfectly done and a sheer delight. We waited eagerly for its distribution here in America. And we went on waiting. There never was any. Nor could any of us make contact with Margaret by mail or phone. The mystery deepened into Agatha Christie proportions, and still remains one. I heard only indirectly of her death. The whole experience was quite an initiation for me as an agent. But the word was out, and I began being contacted by a number of writers who were disillusioned or distrustful of agents in New York. I began finding myself being pressured into a business I had not foreseen. There were no other literary agents in Texas or adjacent states in the southwest at that time, and I recognized the need.

I was next approached by Wade Cutler, a young astrologer who had a unique horoscope reading device and also a book on speed reading, both of which I sold to Prentice Hall Company. In 1966 a Dallas business man, Howard Sparks, had a book—*The Amazing Mail Order Business*—which I got to Frederick Fell for publication that year.

Then Dallas patron of the arts, literature and Texas history, Summerfield G. Roberts, contacted me concerning a project of great interest to him which would become a book of unique value.

He had recently bought the splendid collection of oil portraits of nine men selected from early Texas history and considered most heroic by Dewey Bradford and Maury Maverick, Sr. The two had made the choices when they were Sigma Chi brothers and students at the University of Texas in Austin. They were very concerned because no gallery of true portraits of James Bowie, David Crockett, William Travis, James Fannin, Sam Houston, James

Bonham, Stephen Austin, Mirabeau Lamar, and Ben Milam had ever been painted and assembled for exhibit.

Bradford, the art expert, began his research on just how those men really looked—eyes, hair, complexion, expression. No easy job. Then came the question: Who could paint them realistically from that scanty and often diverse information?

Bradford found the man in 1954, Charles B. Normann, an impoverished Norwegian artist who had come to Austin via Mexico. Bradford saw his talent, took him into his home, and together they worked five years on the portraits. Normann also painted portraits of former Governor James Hogg, William Sydney Porter (O. Henry), and the great sculptress Elisabeth Ney in her studio working on the bust of William Jennings Bryan. He painted those pictures for the Texas State Centennial. His painting "The Reading of the Texas Declaration of Independence" is in the San Jacinto Museum of History.

Normann's historical oil portraits of the nine Texas heroes, painted in the early American technique of their era and placed by Bradford in identical frames of pre-Civil War design, were bought by Summerfield Roberts. Roberts' great-grandfather had settled in San Augustine in 1818 and it was at that home where Sam Houston came to recover from his injury at the Battle of San Jacinto.

Mr. Roberts engaged me to arrange for the "Heroes of Texas" to go on an exhibit tour to various towns and cities over the state, until in 1963 at the request of Governor Price Daniel, the portraits were put on permanent exhibit at the State Archives and Library Building in Austin.

Then I was engaged as agent for a book to feature the portraits with an essay or biographical profile on each man by writers most highly qualified to do so. Those chosen were J. Frank Dobie, Joe B. Frantz, James M. Day, Dorman H. Winfrey, Llerena Friend, Joseph M. Nance, Rupert N. Richardson, Ben Procter and H. Bailey Carroll. I was honored by being asked to write the Introduction, and Paul A. Loftin wrote a Dedication. The book was published in 1964 by Texian Press of Waco in a handsomely produced volume. Robert Davis, a noted historian and collector of Texana himself, was president and editor of Texian Press. Best of all, *Heroes of Texas* has remained in print and continues to sell at a steady pace. What makes it a collector's item is that the chapter on James Bowie by Dobie is the last writing we have from him. He died later that year.

It was a personal and professional joy to have worked on such an exciting project with and for Summerfield Roberts. He was an heroic Texan himself for all he did and gave, which still goes on in the annual thousand dollar literary award in his name to a book on the Republic of Texas period.

Another book I helped to promote, not as agent but because of my great interest and support of Cal Farley's Boys Ranch, was *A Shirttail To Hang To* by Beth Day of *Reader's Digest*. As early as the late 1940s, when I first met and became friends with Cal Farley and his wife Mimi of Amarillo, I have been deeply interested in their great creation of Boys Ranch on the site of the old ghost town

Tascosa. Boys (and now girls at Girls' Town) who have been in trouble from broken or abusive homes are there given the opportunity and guided to become the very best citizens. They attend a fully accredited school where they receive an education superior to many offered elsewhere. Beth wrote her book about Cal and the ranch in 1959. It expressed his practical philosophy, which no one else has matched in action. He and those who have followed him perfected it to endure. The man was unique, and so is his living legacy as Beth and I knew when we met in New York to confer on her book and its promotion. If you can find this book, you will want to go and see for yourself what has grown out of old Tascosa.

Web Maddox, a gentleman of eminence in Fort Worth in law, banking, corporate industry, founder of the Fort Worth Opera Association, and a close friend of General and President Eisenhower, contacted me concerning a book about five Texas outlaws which his friends Amon Carter and James Record of the *Fort Worth Star-Telegram* had long wanted him to write, using their files on the outlaws.

The book had the title *Black Sheep,* which was not so much to indicate a moral judgment as to describe a different wool for history's varied fabric. Mr. Maddox, as his peers knew so well, could and did dip his pen in the indelible ink of the eighteenth-century essayist Joseph Addison. And so, thanks to Maddox, we got a new look at Bonnie and Clyde, Belle Starr, John Wesley Hardin and Sam Bass, "three obstreperous rams and two wild and woolly ewes." Nortex Press in Quanah, Texas, published the book in 1975. It merits reprint, not for its subject but for its style of satire not to be found in today's journalism.

I have grateful memories of sharing many a performance of the Fort Worth Opera season with Web Maddox, most memorably a *Salome* starring Brenda Lewis, who knew what to do with both her voice and those seven veils.

Meanwhile, I had read and most enthusiastically reviewed the great historical novel *Love Is a Wild Assault*, by Elithe Hamilton Kirkland. She had been selected and asked to write that book by the Texas State Historical Association. She was given access to all the factual material of the diary of the heroine—Harriet Moore Page Potter Ames—the Texas State Supreme Court archives, the University of North Carolina Library's Robert Potter papers, and the *Southwestern Law Journal's* report and coverage of the famous and infamous case caused by Colonel Robert Potter, a signer of the Declaration of Independence of the Republic of Texas and Secretary of the Texas Navy, disclaiming Harriet Potter as his wife in his will and naming two women prominent in Austin society to share in his estate.

I came to know Elithe and her husband, a doctor of osteopathy, and visited in their ranch home, Big Sky, near Coleman, Texas, where her Hamilton family had owned the land for many years. She and Dr. Kirkland had each had a previous marriage and a child by those marriages. They were a remarkable couple in so many ways, with interests ranging from literature and history to ranching

and science. Notable, too, was their distrust of banks.
Beyond minimal checking accounts, they would buy a
luxury car or home with thousands of dollars in cash. Elithe
would travel to her various lecturing engagements with
hundreds of dollars. Her son James Beal and I marvel at the
fact that no theft was ever reported. They hid and literally
buried their money in places at home that would seem
almost mischievously chosen.

Elithe's versatility of talents, from her student days
under the teaching of J. Frank Dobie and their work
together on the University of Texas State Radio Network,
to her Distinguished Alumna Award from the University of
North Texas and induction into the Texas Women's Hall
of Fame in 1987, all verify a reputation of unique achievement. As she used to say to me, "We are survivors." It was
typical of her lack of ego to use the plural pronoun.

I was appalled that Doubleday let the book go out of
print after its 1959 publication, which was so successful that
Love Is a Wild Assault became a collector's item and was
being bought at very high prices. Elithe and I discussed this
and she asked me to become her agent and go to New York
to get Doubleday to do something about the matter.

I went and woke them up and the result was a new
reprint edition. In 1977 I sold paperback rights to Avon,
and it went through three mass printings. Then Kirkland's
earlier and first novel, *Divine Average*, a powerful historical
story of a special frontier on the Nueces River and the
Mexican border first published by Little Brown in 1952,
was reprinted by Avon in paperback in 1979.

When all those editions were gone and popular demand continued, a Texas publisher, Shearer of Fredericksburg, reprinted both books in hardback in 1984, and then *Love Is a Wild Assault* in trade paperback in 1991.

Motion picture and television rights were optioned several times on *Love Is a Wild Assault*, but it never got into production for various reasons. However, that potential remains very active both for that book and for *Divine Average,* as both are again under option.

Elithe was author of two later books—*Edge of Disrepute* and *Trellis of Memory*—written under the influence of her husband's interest in parapsychology, but, as I had warned her, their appeal was extremely limited. She also wrote much deeply spiritual poetry on a plateau of thought all her own, and her many musical plays held and continue to hold much promise for production. For readers of all ages was her book *Leet's Christmas,* privately published by White Chapel Press in Wimberley in 1985.

Elithe Kirkland died on January 4, 1992, at her home in Wimberley in the beautiful hill country of Texas which she so loved. A fine and rare poetic stylist in novel writing was lost to our literature and history. It was Frank Dobie who had stated most definitely that she should have been given the Texas Institute of Letters Award, but for some mysterious reason that was never done. When one thinks of some of the books whose writers have received it, the gaffe becomes more blatantly absurd. Kirkland was too big to pay attention to such trivia or be affected by it, and *Love Is a Wild Assault* continues to be the best-selling historical novel over the longest period of time ever to come out of Texas.

Unfortunately the same failure of the Texas Institute of Letters to give appropriate recognition to two other Texas authors honored with national awards has happened in the case of Benjamin Capps and Frank X. Tolbert. One often wonders about such capricious matters.

It was a personal as well as professional delight when the most important historian and authority on the old and true West, its cowboys and outlaws, brands and "lingo," Ramon Adams, came to me to act as agent in 1960. Already famous as the only lexicographer of the American West with his *Cowboy Lingo* published in 1936, and *Western Words, A Dictionary of the Range, Cow Camp and Trail* published by the University of Oklahoma Press in 1944, he would later add to those collections of colorful language *The Cowman Says It Salty,* published by the University of Arizona Press in 1972. The classic *Western Words Dictionary* was reissued by Putnam/Perigee in 1993 under the new title *The Cowboy Dictionary.*

Ramon had never had an agent before coming to me, but he wanted to be relieved of the routine of dealing with publishers so he could concentrate on his writing. His wife never wanted him to have an agent. Allie Adams was a lady averse to anyone getting even ten percent of a royalty. Her hostility was a bit of a problem for all concerned, but Adams had learned to cultivate a deaf ear at home.

He was a remarkable man of many interests whose life story and varied career cry for an adequate biography.

Born in 1890 on a prairie near Houston where he grew up "on a roan pony" among the cowmen of the area, Adams went to Austin College in Sherman and graduated in 1912 from the music department. He went on to teach violin at the University of Arkansas and then played violin in the silent movie theatre orchestras in Fort Worth, Wichita Falls, and Dallas until breaking his wrist cranking a Model T Ford. After that he and his wife went into the candy business in Dallas, both retail and wholesale. One product, a chocolate almond "Burnt Offering," was created for Neiman Marcus.

In 1955, however, Adams concentrated on his third and lasting career—writing the history, bibliography, and lexicography of the cattle country and its people. He wrote twenty-four books and never received a rejection from any publisher to the day he died in April of 1976. If that isn't a record, I don't know of one. Notable, too, was that Adams wrote the first biography of Charles Russell in 1948.

My work with him and for him came in his later years when I handled *The Old-Time Cowhand,* published by Macmillan in 1961, and *From the Pecos to the Powder, a Cowboy's Autobiography As Told to Ramon F. Adams by Bob Kennon,* published by the University of Oklahoma Press in 1965.

The library of western Americana he collected was of great value. He sold most of it to Senator Bill Blakely, and later his widow sold the rest of it before her death in 1987. Of course all of it should have been properly preserved as a collection in an appropriate university library of high repute.

In 1989 I announced reprints of *The Old-Time Cow-hand* by the University of Nebraska Press in both hard and soft cover, and *Burrs Under the Saddle, More Burrs Under the Saddle* and *From the Pecos to the Powder* from the University of Oklahoma Press. There is no end of the trail made by Ramon Adams. I am proud to have gone part of the way with him, and exult in the continued interest in and sales of his books today.

One of the most interesting projects that came to me as literary agent was in the mid-1970s. A brilliant investigative reporter, Gifford Guy Gibson, writer and editor for Pacific News Service of San Francisco whose feature articles had been in newspapers coast to coast, was covering a sensational court case in Dallas in December 1975. It was the first known jury trial on the child custody rights of a homosexual parent, Mary Jo Risher, the mother.

In collaboration with her, he was writing a book about her experiences, a book of considerable importance. At that time the gay and lesbian subject had been written about only by the English poet and novelist Radclyffe Hall in *Well of Loneliness* in 1928, and much later the New York journalist and novelist Laura Hobson in *Consenting Adult* in 1975.

I contacted Doubleday on the Gibson-Risher book, and they published it in 1977 under the title *By Her Own Admission*. It got excellent reviews from critics courageous enough to write them. Today it would be a bestseller. A couple of decades can make a difference in a century which has moved as fast sociologically as this one. ABC contracted for a motion picture which was made in the fall of 1978 by Viacom starring Gena Rowlands, Jane Alexander and Ned Beatty. It continues on television reruns and is available on video cassette. The shock of the subject has vanished with the years and the changes in our society. C'est la vie. But the drama remains intact. In fact, in 1992 a contract was made with a San Diego theatre company for a stage play based upon the book.

The art of translation has always been a challenge, and few have been as successful as Barnett Shaw of Dallas. Expert in French and highly talented as a character actor from his student years at the University of Texas in Austin, he played in many of the Dallas Theatre Center productions. He spent much time in France and became especially interested in the hilarious farces by Georges Feydeau and their potential for American theatre audiences. His translations were remarkable in skill, and soon *A Flea in Her Ear* was in production by theatre companies from California across country to Broadway.

As agent I attended to the Samuel French Company publication of the play, but I was even more interested in Barnett's expertise in translating the great Alexandre Dumas père, famed the world over for his *Three Musketeers* and *Count of Monte Cristo.* This gifted Texas linguist concentrated on Dumas's work as dramatist, which equaled what Dumas wrote as novelist but was less known in America.

We got the attention of Frederick Ungar of New York who read the Shaw translation and adaptation of four

Dumas plays which had so delighted the Comédie-Française nineteenth-century audiences and remained in repertory long after the turn of the century. The result was the 1979 publication by the Ungar Company of the book *The Great Lover and Other Plays*. The other three plays included were *Kean*, so titled for the noted English actor, *Young King Louis*, and *Three Interludes for the Love Doctor*, which Dumas wrote for a Molière birthday.

Barnett Shaw also translated Dumas's marvelous memoir about his château and menagerie there, *Histoire de Mes Bêtes*, but to our great regret I could not get it published. The French government, however, awarded him the Medal of Chevalier dans L'Ordre des Arts et Lettres.

There are many regrets in agenting when one has a truly fine manuscript and cannot find a publisher, or when a book is published and never gets to the full potential of its market.

The latter was an experience I had to endure in 1983 when the Fred Lowery autobiography, *Whistling in the Dark,* was published by Pelican Company. Fred was a national celebrity as a whistler with the bands of Vincent Lopez and Horace Heidt in the Big Band era. His virtuosity as a whistler matched any flutist. In fact, his unique musical gift was more often likened to that of the sound of the piccolo, which is an octave higher than the ordinary flute. Fred Lowery was legally blind, which was another distinction.

I knew of him. Who didn't if you listened to radio and his recordings of "Indian Love Call," "The High and the

Mighty," "La Golondrina" and so many others. We all had read newspaper reports, too, on his performance at Carnegie Hall and at the White House for President Franklin Roosevelt.

I had never met him personally, however, until he and his wife Gracie came to me in the late 1970s. They were living at that time in the east Texas town of Jacksonville. The Big Band era was over, unfortunately, and there was nothing rock 'n roll about Fred Lowery. Nor country western. His whistling was pure lyric melody. Engagements were few.

They had a big camper, and Gracie drove them everywhere with the skill of a trucker. Their son Fred, who lived in Houston, had urged Lowery to dictate his remarkable memoir into a tape recorder. Then long-time friend John R. McDowell, Indianapolis journalist, went to work to edit it into a book manuscript.

It was fascinating to read this inspiring human interest story that somehow bubbled with his own sense of humor about a handicapped boy orphaned at two years old who came out of the east Texas cotton fields to the Texas School for the Blind in Austin. There a teacher of great insight and foresight recognized his unique talent and started him on his career as concert whistler.

His story was star-studded, with Harry James (who contributed a Foreword), Glenn Miller, Mary Martin, Bing Crosby, Judy Garland, Perry Como, Bob Hope, to name a few with whom he shared experiences and adventures in show business. It was a sheer delight to read, and infused with the dynamic personality of the man.

Then bad things began to happen. John McDowell was suddenly stricken and died, and while Lowery was on a promotional tour to autograph books he had a heart attack and died. No national promotion was continued. The only good thing that remains to be said is that *Whistling in the Dark* is still in print and available, plus it has great potential for television.

One of the most valuable books of Americana which I handled as agent was *Big Thicket Legacy* by Campbell and Lynn Loughmiller. For that book the Loughmillers had gone into the primeval wilderness in southeast Texas known as the Big Thicket, a wonderland of botany, biology, geology to be penetrated and explored in safety only with a professional guide or native. A few of those natives remain in primitive isolation there, all of them related, some of incredible age, others the great-grandchildren of original settlers. It was the stories of their lives that the Loughmillers taped, just as they talked in their own regional vernacular, for an oral history comparable in value only to the ballad collections by John and Alan Lomax. It was and is fascinating reading as published by the University of Texas Press in 1977. Mr. Loughmiller died December 4, 1993, at their home in Whitehouse, Texas, but their book is kept in print for readers today.

Another book that was a pleasure to work with as agent was Bill Porterfield's *A Loose Herd of Texans,* published by Texas A & M University Press in 1978. This selected collection of Porterfield's feature stories and essays for various newspapers and magazines is still in print and continues to be enjoyed by all who appreciate quality of style and originality in the word pictures of one-of-a-kind characters.

For the radio industry I was able to place the monumental *Radio Format Conundrum* by Edd Routt, Fredric Weiss and James McGrath for Hastings House publication. Then when *The Dallas Morning News* columnist Bob St. John's splendid book on the world and way of life of rodeo people, *On Down the Road,* published by Prentice-Hall in 1977, was allowed to go out of print, I arranged for its reprint by Eakin Press. No other book on rodeo is ever likely to equal it.

I also went to Eakin in Austin with another book of very special importance by the man who, as an individual, was leading the fight in Texas and America for environmental protection—Edward C. (Ned) Fritz. The book was an all-out frontal attack against clear-cutting our forests. It was written from the most thorough and authentic knowledge of a natural scientist and with the passion of a trial lawyer, which was Ned's profession.

Perhaps in fear of offending certain industrial support, state university presses backed away from publishing *Sterile Forest, The Case Against Clear-cutting.* It was published by Eakin Press in 1983. Dr. Fritz gave all royalties to the Texas Committee on Natural Resources. A year later, in October 1984, President Ronald Reagan signed into law a bill protecting over 34,000 acres of East Texas timberland as a federal wilderness area. I like to think that this potent little book of 271 pages by a dedicated conservationist blazed a trail that began to lead us toward some wisdom about our world. Like Dr. Fritz, and not irreverently, I often wonder if it were not a divine mistake for man to have been given dominion over the earth.

My only venture as agent in the religious field was with the books by my friend Dr. Robert Kahn, Rabbi (now Emeritus) of Temple Emanu-El in Houston and a past president of the Central Conference of American Rabbis. For many years he wrote a most popular weekly column "Lessons For Life" for the *Houston Chronicle* and broadcast a series of sermonettes on radio.

In 1963 Doubleday published a Book Club edition of his *Lessons for Life* as he expanded those nuggets of wisdom. Then a year later they published Kahn's *The Ten Commandments for Today,* which Pyramid reprinted in 1974 in paperback for their Family Library. In 1972 Word Books published his book *The Letter and the Spirit* in which Biblical laws are related to contemporary ethics and the moral standards so endangered and abused in today's society. If ever a book needed reprinting today, this one does.

Another book of merit in Texas frontier fiction was the novel *Time of Passion* by Sondra Shands of Brownsville. Published in 1983 by a local company (now extinct) favored by the author for personal reasons, the book received good reviews but incompetent and inadequate distribution, as I had feared and warned. Agents are not always allowed to be in control.

For older children, especially girls in the young adult age of early teens, good books flavored with our great

Southwest are rare. But a writer I know in Mt. Vernon, Texas, Laurel Jean Pamplin, an excellent historian of the old Western cattle trail, wrote such a book. The story, a true one, of a twelve-year-old girl who masqueraded as a cowboy to go on a cattle drive from Texas into New Mexico became the novel *Masquerade on the Western Trail,* published by Eakin in 1991. Diversity is good for an agent, for there can and should be quality in every genre of writing, and young readers need it most of all to counteract television.

My only other venture as agent in the children's field had been earlier in 1970 for my friend Luise Putcamp, Jr., and her delightful little book *The Christmas Carol Miracle,* published by Abingdon Press. Originally it was a short story in *Good Housekeeping* magazine in December, 1954, and won a Christopher Award the following year under the title "The Miracle at Derrick, Texas."

In 1970, Mrs. Alvin M. Owsley of Dallas, widow of the Past Commander of the American Legion and former ambassador, in turn, to Rumania, Ireland, Denmark, asked me to meet with Marion Adams of Indianapolis who was writing the authorized biography of Colonel Owsley. I did so, and the result was the vibrant life story of a most colorful career, in the book *Alvin M. Owsley of Texas, Apostle of Americanism* published by Texian Press in 1971. General Mark Clark contributed the Foreword. The book holds much value and interest as both biography and history, and, of course, is now a collector's item.

A book manuscript of special importance in military and aviation history was brought to my attention in 1968 by

Captain Robert Gruenhagen of the Texas Air National Guard. From Montana and the Air National Guard where he was aircraft maintenance officer for the 120th fighter group in Great Falls, he had come to live in Arlington, Texas. For several years he had been researching here and in England all the detail about the Second World War's most famous fighter plane, the P-51 Mustang.

His book *Mustang* had the interest of a new publishing company in Dallas, Genesis Press, with Arco Publishing Company in New York as distributor. A prominent public relations agent in Dallas, Judy Bonner, added her pressure on the author to go with Genesis. Most reluctantly I agreed. That was the first and last book from Genesis Press. *Mustang* deserved a more qualified publisher for its flight in 1967. Again, I must repeat, an agent is not always in control.

Such memories of past work give way to the contemporary and how in the summer of 1993 I had a talk with an old friend of many years, Stanley Marcus, a friendship inherited from our parents. I told him that his weekly columns for *The Dallas Morning News* were so different from other columns because of his variety and scope of thinking on such a wide range of multiple subjects and interests that a selected collection of them would make a book of much potential for the reading public. He agreed, and the result was that I became his agent and we contracted with the University of North Texas Press for the book's publication in 1995, with the title *The Viewpoints of Stanley Marcus: A Ten-Year Perspective*. Stanley has been called a "renaissance man," and that description is valid because of the breadth and depth of his expertise in business and his scholarly appreciation of the arts, both in collecting and in his participation as writer and publisher.

In that same productive summer of 1993 came the pleasure of restoring the tasty delights of Frank Tolbert's *A Bowl of Red* into a new edition with Texas A&M University Press for 1994 publication. The reprint was garnished with a Foreword by that grande dame of West Texas ranching in the Big Bend, Hallie Stillwell, author of *I'll Gather My Geese*. The Tolbert book on chili has been steaming and bubbling through reprints since 1972.

From the University of Queensland Press in Australia will come a book of personal and inspirational adventure by a remarkable young pilot, Captain Rod Lewin of the Delta connection, Atlantic Southeast Airlines, whom I have worked with as agent ever since he came from Australia to Dallas and wrote the manuscript of the book. Entitled *Steel Spine, Iron Will*, it was printed in 1991 in limited edition by Taylor Publishing Company and attracted much attention for its true story of this Australian flyer who crashed on a test flight, became paralyzed and doomed to a wheel chair and overcame that condition to come to Texas, marry here and continue a most successful career in the air. It is a memoir of guts and humor and high altitude entertainment. Whatever the title change in Australia, that publication will undoubtedly attract more editions in other countries and inevitably television production will follow.

As an agent as well as advisor and sometimes personal friend of many writers for many years, I have always warned them not to let their frustration drive them to self-publish or, worse yet, fall victim to the blandishments and advertising of "vanity presses." If they do, after they have exhausted the market of selling copies to family and friends, they simply have to become salesmen or saleswomen of their product, which the bookstores and jobbers seldom welcome (except on consignment) and the professional reviewers ignore. Most poets, however, have been left with no other way to go, if they are ever to get into print today. Only in the western states from Montana to Texas, where the so-called cowboy poets flourish, does the singing word still reach its public.

Of course it's nothing new for authors to get out and promote their books in every way they can, as, for example, even an author as successful as Irving Stone always did. But Mr. Stone could *talk* and would never have resorted to the utter boredom of reading "excerpts" as so many do today at what can only be called literary side shows. Now with publishers doing less and less for their authors, the writers are having to do more and more. Maybe that is why there is not enough time for good writing.

There is, though, another hope emerging now on the literary scene, and it has come and continues to come from our African-American writers, for example, the powerful pen and voice of Maya Angelou and Nobel Prize winner Toni Morrison and their many peers who have evolved through two arduous centuries here. In fact, I see much of the future of our American literature coming from the minds and out of the hearts and souls of our African-American and our Hispanic writers, such as Lionel Garcia, in both fiction and nonfiction, as well as a renaissance of poetry. In this connection I remember the words of Reverend James McLaughlin of St. James AME Church in Dallas at a 1993 lecture program event, "Before we were allowed to learn to read and write, we *sang* in the cotton fields." That was indeed the source from which a new literature grew in America.

In the winter of 1994 Dr. Valerie Hotchkiss, director of Bridwell Library, initiated and conducted a program event and exhibit for African-American History Month honoring Black Seminarians of Perkins School of Theology at Southern Methodist University since 1952. My list of first editions of twentieth-century Black literature from my collection at Bridwell was also presented. Already there were my copies of Alex Haley's *Roots* and Richard Wright's *Native Son*, but the new list included this interesting variety of books from 1958 through 1993: *The Lonesome Road*, by J. Saunders Redding; *Jubilee*, by Margaret Walker; *The Black West*, by William Loren Katz; *Black Defender of America*, by Robert Ewell Greene; *Black Women Writers* from Anchor Press/Doubleday; *The Chaneysville Incident*, by David Bradley; *The Shaping of Black America*, by Lerone Bennett; *Capitol Hill in Black and White*, by Robert Parker; *The Wolf and the Buffalo*, by Elmer Kelton; *The Legend of John Brown: A Biography and History*, by Richard Owen

Boyer; *Render Me My Song: African American Women Writers from Slavery to the Present*, by Sandi Russell; *Love in Black and White: The Triumph of Love over Prejudice and Taboo*, by Mark Mathabane; *Waiting in Line at the Drugstore and Other Writings of James Thomas Jackson*, collected by June Acosta; *From Slave to Statesman: The Legacy of Joshua Houston, Servant to Sam Houston*, by Patricia Smith Prather and Jane Clements Monday; *All God's Children Need Traveling Shoes*, by Maya Angelou; *The Mixed Blessing*, by Helen Van Slyke; *Autobiography of Miss Jane Pittman* by Ernest Gaines (paperback printing after the CBS-TV special production); *"I Have a Dream," Quotations of Martin Luther King, Jr.*, by Lotte Hoskins; *Marva Collins' Way*, by Marva Collins and Civia Tamarkin.

Like Topsy the agenting work has grown, and to me there is a satisfying sense of helping writers to get published and to help worthy publishers get writers of value. The time invested seldom pays off in dollars and cents, but when one loves books as I do, one is as foolish and impractical as any other lover.

QED
Quod erat demonstrandum

There will always be books because there will always be writers. As Ernest Hemingway wrote to Charles Scribner in 1940, "I have to write to be happy, whether I get paid for it or not. It's a hell of a disease to be born with."

The act of creation to express and record what we see, hear, feel and think is a most personal compulsion, coming solely from within, and this is as natural in the human being as the need for food and water. In fact, such basic necessities are related as we forever seek to nourish more than our bodies. The heart, the mind, the soul know hunger too.

We want to leave something behind us about our world and what happens in it and about the men and women who make or let it happen and cope with it and so are of special interest to us. Thus does the writing of history and biography emerge and evolve.

As I see it, however, it is the novelist who can and does reflect and reveal society most truly. Scientists can take us into outer space, but it is the good novelist and certainly the great ones who can take us into inner space, that world of mysteries and wonders within ourselves. Always the novelists have given us the confrontation of good and evil. What is new today and bodes ill for the future is that too many novels focus only on evil and depravity. Unlike the great novelists, this new commercial breed are not equal to presenting characters who can cope with evil.

Much of this decline into trash has come from a completely false definition of realism. The word is applied only to the lowest levels of behavior and conditions. Realism is much bigger than that. It encompasses *all* of reality on every level, the good and the bad, the beautiful and the ugly, and the chemistry of their combination in human nature. That ancient figure of mythology, the centaur—half man, half beast—may still be the best symbol of realism for all of us. But we want the whole picture of ourselves and our society, not just half of it, the worst half. There must be balance in any art.

Few writers of our time knew that better than Louis L'Amour. I remember him telling me once how he walked the miles and rode the trails he wrote about. He could see the men and women take shape out of the land and hear their words to convey to us. And so he did. I would know a Sackett anywhere and be aware of "the lonesome gods" when they whisper in the desert night to the people who once heard them. When a reader can say that, he or she has experienced realism in a book.

I fear that my generation of writers, readers, and book-lovers may be the last in this century whose approach was directed to the humanities, especially in the art of literature. Our study of the story and stories of life was for fulfillment, not in the hedonist sense nor as a Johnny-one-note formula technician. Forgotten or perhaps not even known today is the great nineteenth-century art critic John Ruskin and his trinity of values, "the true, the good, the beautiful," but the yearning remains as we try to adjust to the false, the base, the ugly—and cannot.

It no doubt has been noted that the names of Larry McMurtry and Katherine Anne Porter are among some others missing in these pages. My reason is not to denigrate their talents nor be unaware of them, but to evaluate in a more truthful perspective than has sometimes been done. For example, it has been written in several books that they were the first writers to come out of Texas and gain national recognition, and that is totally erroneous. Frank Dobie was the first for not only national but international acclaim when he was invited to England to teach and receive an honorary degree at Cambridge University in 1943. In 1959 Elithe Kirkland's novel of early Texas history *Love Is a Wild Assault* was acclaimed in *The New York Times* and *New York Herald Tribune* reviews and across the country, plus even more from the critics in Germany and Spain for the translated editions in those countries.

Like Michener, McMurtry's early books were of great promise, but commercial success diverted that promise. Historical authenticity with McMurtry was too often sacrificed to melodrama, notably in *Lonesome Dove* and its inevitable sequel(s). His utterly inept prophecy that Frank Dobie's books would not outlast another generation could have the backlash of applying to his own. As Mr. Dobie once observed, "Intellectual integrity seems to me as rare in American writing as in politics."

In the case of Porter, her finely and tightly spun gossamer quality prose in novellas, short stories and the novel *Ship of Fools* was infected by the publicity she generated. When a writer becomes elevated to a position for reasons other than literary, it's unfortunate. I have never seen why a Texas connection was forced upon her when she forever denied it for her own psychiatric reasons. She was simply better at writing than at living—not an uncommon situation.

A real writer is born. Journalism can be taught, but I doubt that great writing ever can be, despite all the courses offered in colleges and universities. Such courses can be helpful, but that is all. The gift comes more from a genie than a gene. A notable exception, of course, was Dumas père and Dumas fils.

Often I have told those who want to be professional writers that the best training is to read books time-tested to be the best in their genres. That experience of reading good writing is like exposure to an environment. You absorb that quality in a natural process, an osmosis.

Of primary importance is the gifted ability to write children's books. I firmly believe that the best present to give any child is a book to discover the magic in it. Only from children who read can come a generation of readers. Otherwise illiteracy gains its frightening momentum.

Fine writers in all literary categories have their personal oddities, of course, just like other folks. I recall, for instance, that William Humphrey once wrote to me declining an invitation to attend a Dallas book and author affair to honor him with a substantial award because he hated the thought of returning to his home state for anything. However, that did not prevent him from accepting the award and cashing the check sent to him. The fact remains that he can write superbly well, whether about people or fishing. I doubt if that opening sentence of Daphne du Maurier's, "Last night I dreamt I went to Manderley again," has more initial impact than the scene and mood depicted on the first page of Humphrey's novel *Home from the Hill.*

I have also committed the cardinal sin of by-passing the icons William Faulkner, Philip Roth and John Updike, but not because I am unaware of them. In Roth's case I can only say that a confused mind and emotional imbalance seldom produce more than publicity. In Updike's case, his brilliance has been for and within the confines of a literary cult. As for Faulkner, despite his Nobel Prize, to me he stays where he forever was—in Yoknapatawpha County. In his work we have the expression of a regional malaise, and that too imposes its limits; when one thinks of him, one thinks of Mississippi in a way its residents today might prefer would be otherwise.

Our English language is so beautiful and so rich when it is written for its full orchestration of meaning as well as sound. The words can be simple, but the moods they convey in major and minor keys offer a writer the choice of every instrument to express feeling and thought and even action. Often we hear it said that words are inadequate. They are not. It is a matter of vocabulary and taking time to find the right word, for there always is one.

It seems to me that only French has equal wealth of choice for the writer. We have but to compare the other bodies of world literature to see that this is so, though every language and every dialect has words utterly unique for their special meaning, which is why we borrow from each other as needed. To see and hear any language mutilated by ignorance is to witness destruction of the *art* of communication. No science can replace an art. We need to remember that, and we need more writers to remind us of it by the *way* they write, not just *what* they write.

The effect of movie production based on books can be of so much help to reading. Screen productions with directors wise enough to stay true to the book cause a flurry of sending viewers to bookstores and libraries, as publishers have learned to provide for now.

I can remember that earliest movie made of *Last of the Mohicans* and how it stimulated people to get back to a writer they had almost forgotten about—James Fenimore Cooper. Later it was sheer delight to see how perfectly the novel *Rebecca* was first filmed and also *The Forsyte Saga, Gone With the Wind, Winds of War, War and Remembrance, The Thorn Birds* and *The Sacketts*, and more recently the re-discovery of Virginia Woolf and her *Orlando* and Edith Wharton's *Age of Innocence*, and her classic *Ethan Frome* was also filmed earlier to perfection, though a more recent one for television was not. Both films sparked resurgence of interest in reading those great books, and of course the same was true of the utterly delightful *Gigi* introducing so many to the short stories of the brilliant Colette.

Only a minority of Americans can read Yiddish, but even so we all learned that the great popular folk opera *Fiddler on the Roof* came right out of the stories by Sholem Aleichem, translated from that old language of eastern European Jewry. The great theatre and screen productions of *Henry V* and *Macbeth* and *Hamlet* sent at least a few folks to read or re-read Shakespeare. Because of the impact of stage and screen on such a huge public, those media can be of more help than any others to reading the books which are their source.

I have never thought that television or video-audio cassettes are of any major threat to books. Those media are too dependent on books. Similarly, what would become of music if all the scores in print were gone? Momentary entertainment is one thing, but satisfaction of the on-going needs within us is another. Ergo, books—good ones, great ones. Algonquin Books of Chapel Hill editor Robert Rubin recently penned a memorable sentence, "A good book has a little eternity in it." The feel of such a book in our hands holds an aura of permanence which only vandalism of one sort or another could destroy.

One of the most atrocious threats to books is the act of banning or burning them. We have seen this happen for centuries since the great library at Alexandria was destroyed in Egypt and the world lost the biggest body of ancient literature ever assembled. Our own twentieth century saw the German Nazi desecration of books by great Jewish writers. Even here in America there are pockets of such evil which erupt at intervals. I will admit that there are times when my own hands itch to set a match to some of the junk I see published, but I compromise, trusting time to sift the trash out and away, as it does to those who produce it. I take comfort in that thought.

Few are the publishers astute enough to know what the reading public always wants and hungers for, as when Marjorie Rawlings wrote *The Yearling* and Erich Segal wrote *Love Story* and Sheila Burnford wrote *The Incredible Journey* and Rosamunde Pilcher wrote *The Shell Seekers* and Elizabeth Hailey wrote *A Woman of Independent Means* and Robert Waller wrote *Bridges of Madison County* and Jane Roberts Wood wrote *The Train to Estelline* and its two sequels, to name a few examples. Most of us want a story, short or long, that feeds our spirit, is unashamed of sentiment, reveals a truth or echoes a dream and strikes a chord in those of us who still have a song left in us—a song, not a dirge or a scream.

For over half a century I have watched our literary parade and participated in it. I see more writing of poor

BRIDWELL LIBRARY

AND

MR. AND MRS. DECHERD TURNER

INVITE YOU TO GREET

MISS EVELYN OPPENHEIMER

AT THE BEGINNING OF THE TWENTY-FIFTH YEAR

OF

HER RADIO BROADCAST

OF

BOOK REVIEWS AND AUTHOR INTERVIEWS.

SUNDAY, JANUARY 20, 1974
4-6 P.M.

BRIDWELL LIBRARY
6005 BISHOP BOULEVARD
SOUTHERN METHODIST UNIVERSITY

Invitation from Bridwell Library at Southern Methodist University and Mr. and Mrs. Decherd Turner to celebrate the beginning of Evelyn Oppenheimer's twenty-fifth year of radio broadcast in 1974.

quality in print now in the closing decade of this century than ever before. Why?

Time has caught up with us, and the time is one of decadence. Historically it is cyclical, coming toward the finale of every civilization. People simply self-destruct from their own stupidity no matter how clever they seem to be. Academic degrees and hi-tech do not always include and improve upon common sense. There should be a C.S. degree offered somewhere. We can get into outer space, but we cannot get along with each other here on earth. We

*Evelyn with Decherd Turner at the Bridwell Library cutting
the cake.*

turn our backs on all the great teachers such as Moses and Jesus, and pay them only lip service once a week.

Our literature mirrors the sick results. A few writers, too few, remain the exception—those of the deep insights and big perspective to see beyond the gutter to the horizon. They know the value of the tradition they inherit as writers not only of and for *their* time but for *all* time. The writer who confines himself to only one aspect of his subject or one facet of a character is of no consequence and certainly without knowledge of our human and social complexity. This is not a dogmatic statement but literary fact.

Often today I am asked what I think about the trend of huge warehouse-size bookstores under even more huge corporate or conglomorate ownership. My answer is that I don't care about the size of the stores but only about their content, and if the management and staff know the difference between Danielle Steele and Daniel Webster. Books are all that matter—all kinds, old and new—in a bookstore.

Of course I miss the little bookshop, cozy, intimately redolent of the joys of reading and the sharing of those joys. Such shops were the nests that nurtured us. But wherever there are books a natural rendezvous evolves for persons who exchange their thoughts about them with each other. Moreover, one can always find a corner where one can be alone with the pages that take you out of that corner and out of your own limitations.

So let the bookstores be big or small. To paraphrase old Omar: A Book of Verses underneath the Roof, a Jug (coffee, tea, or milk), a Loaf of Bread and Thou, Oh

Readers. . . . Paradise indeed as the Persian scholar defined it. I can add only one thing more—that the Book be as affordable as the Bread.

I have read thousands of books and loved hundreds of them. A favorite to take to a desert island? First, let's find a desert island. Is there one left today? Making such a choice of a book like that is a lot like getting married. You love the person. You may even be "in love" with the person. But the commitment to be with that person day in and day out "in sickness and in health till death do you part"? That calls for more thought than it usually gets. So, too, with the book to take to that desert island. I keep on changing my mind. That may be why I have never married (though coming dangerously close several times)—nor found and gone to the island—yet.

A book lover collects books all his or her life. As a reviewer, of course, I received many from publishers and authors. Many more I have bought. Some have been gifts. Nothing ever matched the bargain I got once at a book sale in Chicago, a lovely little *Canticle of the Sun of St. Francis of Assisi* in its English version by Matthew Arnold and published in 1907 by Premier Press of Duffield & Company, which I bought for a penny!

Gradually, inevitably, I began defining the focus of my library. First and foremost was quality of writing, whatever category of the book or nationality of the writer. Not to have a big shelf of Voltaire, Anatole France, de Maupassant, Romain Rolland, Emile Zola, George Sand, Dumas père et fils, Flaubert, Balzac, Colette, Saint Exupéry, Edmond Rostand would be a most dismal gap. After all, the French dipped their pens into a magical ink for modern literature.

A smaller shelf for Russia and Germany and the depths of despair and passion pin-pointed by their Chekhov, Tolstoy, Heine, Schiller, Dostoevski, Goethe, Mann, Pasternak.

England required many shelves, beginning with several editions of the Master Bard of Stratford, and then coming up through the centuries of poetry, biography, history, fiction, essays, drama.

Ireland I left with Joyce in his bog and those mired down in it with him. Instead, I took and take that literary leprechaun George Bernard Shaw and William Yeats.

I was and am grateful to Australia for Morris West, Nevil Shute and Colleen McCullough.

More and more of my own special interest fastened on western Americana and on Texana in particular. However, there were many exceptions as I read northeast with Edith Wharton, John Marquand, Louis Auchincloss, Herman Wouk, Robert Frost, Edna St. Vincent Millay, John Masefield, Dorothy Parker, Walter Lord.

Gradually I began to realize that many books in my overflowing library had escalating commercial as well as literary value. I was not just a book lover, but unintentionally I had become a collector, and apartment living has inadequate space and security for first editions, many of them autographed and personally inscribed.

I was also engaged in another collection, one not at all professional and of no value except to me because it is memory-laden: stones and shells I have found wherever I

Evelyn giving a lecture at the Bridwell Library on "The Challenge of Collecting Modern Literature."

Evelyn stands with part of the more than seven hundred books in The Evelyn Oppenheimer Collection of general modern literature, housed in the Bridwell Library, Southern Methodist University. The collection also contains manuscripts, ephemera, copies and tapes of forty-five years of radio broadcast book reviews.

Evelyn and author Marshall Terry exchange literary talk at the Bridwell Library lecture.

Evelyn at the tribute to her given by the Dallas Chapter of the Women's National Book Association which had nominated Evelyn for the National Book Woman of the Year Award. Seated to the left is Jane Roberts Wood who took part in the tribute to Evelyn.

have been. Chunks of snow white marble mined from that mountain of it at Marble, Colorado, and rocks that glimmer with Fool's Gold from wilderness trails to towering Fossil Ridge, rocks of pink granite from our Texas hill country mountain—the same granite of unique color used to build the state capitol and the Galveston sea wall—and a fine hunk of stone aglow with native turquoise from a magic mountain near Cimarron, New Mexico. Then there are my shells of all kinds and shapes and forms from the shores of Padre Island and California and Indianola, Cornwall and Capri, coral from Nassau, each a mystery story never to be written of how they came to be where I found them.

It was in the 1970s that the director of Bridwell Library at Southern Methodist University at that time, Dr. Dechard Turner, asked and urged me to consider having my collection of books take its place among the great special collections at Bridwell, which is world famous for its rare books and incunabula in the religious field for Perkins School of Theology. My collection would be the first for the rare in general modern literature. I agreed, and so the Evelyn Oppenheimer Collection began at Bridwell Library, and I continue adding to it at regular intervals from my home library. Over seven hundred books, plus manuscripts by twentieth-century authors and artists of a quality which I believe can endure, ephemera, copies and tapes of forty-five years of radio broadcast book reviews comprise my collection at Bridwell at present. Of interest, too, is my special collection of children's books given to the rare books library at the University of North Texas.

Among American authors in this collection whose work I believe will continue to increase in value through the years are Ramon Adams, Louis Auchincloss, Louis L'Amour, Oliver LaFarge, Sherwood Anderson, Pearl Buck, Maxwell Anderson, Edith Wharton, Rachel Carson, Theodore Dreiser, Benjamin Capps, Willa Cather, Mari Sandoz, Bruce Catton, A. B. Guthrie, Jr., Eugene O'Neill, Saul Bellow, Amy Lowell, J. Frank Dobie, Edna Ferber, Edna St. Vincent Millay, Robert Frost, Alex Haley, Fred Gipson, Ernest Hemingway, Paul Horgan, William Humphrey, Joseph Wood Krutch, Tom Lea, Sinclair Lewis, Edwin Arlington Robinson, Christopher Morley, William Shirer, Carson McCullers, Dorothy Parker, William Saroyan, John Steinbeck, Wallace Stegner, Irving Stone, Will Durant, Mark Twain, Thomas Wolfe, Thornton Wilder, James Baldwin, Richard Wright, Herman Wouk, Leon Uris, Barbara Tuchman, Antonia Frazer, Tony Hillerman, Doris Kearns Goodwin, George Sessions Perry, David Lavender, Frank X. Tolbert, Elmer Kelton, William Owens, Chaim Potok, James Michener, John Graves, Allan Bloom, Daniel Boorstin, Roy Bedichek, William Prescott Webb, David Westheimer, Maya Angelou, Harnett Kane, Tennessee Williams, Eudora Welty, and for her one book, Margaret Mitchell—one can be enough if it is good enough—and this is true, too, for Elithe Hamilton Kirkland and her two Texas historical novels.

Currently-producing Texas writers who are also in my collection at Bridwell Library, whose books I believe have the potential to endure and hold interest and value for the future in their various genres are Jane Roberts Wood,

Marshall Terry, Carlton Stowers, Robert Flynn, Clay Reynolds, A. C. Greene, Leonard Sanders, Lionel Garcia, Elizabeth Forsythe Hailey, Pete A. Y. Gunter, C. W. Smith, Judy Alter, and, I hope, a book or two of mine.

It's no gamble to recognize the value of a book, manuscript or scroll from centuries ago. It *is* a gamble to prophesy from our time for the future, a gamble more exciting than any game or lottery. When we tire of hearing the angels sing, let us meet in Heaven's own library a hundred or so years from now and see how right or wrong I have been. Among us up there will be Thomas Carlyle, of course, and I intend to ask him to repeat the following part of the great lecture he gave on "The Choice of Books" at the University of Edinburgh over a century ago:

> One remark more about your reading. I do not know whether it has sufficiently brought home to you that there are two kinds of books. When a man is reading on any kind of subject, you will find that there is a division of good books and bad books—there is a good kind of book and a bad kind of book. I remind you that it is a very important consideration at present. It casts aside altogether the idea that people have that if they are reading any book—that if an ignorant man is reading any book, he is doing rather better than nothing at all. I entirely call that in question. I even venture to deny it.
>
> It would be much better and safer would he have no concern with books at all than with

some of them. You know these are my views. But he will learn also that a number of books were written by a supreme, noble kind of people—not a very great number. In short I conceive that books are like men's souls—divided into sheep and goats.

Whatever you may learn here, you are to remember that the object is not particular knowledge—that you are to get only technical perfections. There is a higher aim, especially among those intended for literary, for speaking pursuits—the sacred profession. You are ever to bear in mind the acquisition of what may be called wisdom—namely, sound appreciation and just decision as to all the objects that come round about you, and the habit of behaving with justice and wisdom. In short, great is the value of wisdom. It cannot be exaggerated. The highest achievement of man—"Blessed is he that getteth understanding." That, I believe, may be missed very easily; but never more easily than now, I think. If that is a failure, all is a failure. Wise books—as much as possible good books, and the exclusion of all kinds of clap-trap books which merely excite the astonishment of foolish people.

Amen, Thomas, Amen.

Lagniappe

$\mathcal{S}$ometimes a writer, squirrel-like, has a few acorns hidden away to share if and when the spirit moves him or her. And so I offer the following poems from my book *Legend and Other Poems*, and a short story, "The Green Conscience," which won a Southwest Writers Award. I hope that they will be as enjoyable to read as they were for me to write.

Evelyn Oppenheimer

Epistle

Such lovely things we share, my dear—
A moonlit chapel door,
Pigeons winging in the dusk,
Autumn leaves adrift and soaring,
The scented snow of pale gardenia blooms,
Lilacs breathing in the night,
A quiet, dreaming lily-pond,
Hours hushed by soft rainfall,
The strong sweet silence of a kiss;
And those long walks into the infinite
Beyond and yet within ourselves where
Beauty binds and blesses us and,
Whispering low, confides her secrets
To our love till they are one and
We a consecrated part forever of
These lovely things we share, my dear.

Fragment

"Do you believe in fairies?"
Asked Peter Pan of me;
"Yes!" I cried and wondered
Why he laughed and ran from me.

Footnote

Yesterday, so tender and true;
Today, a stranger
Yet, both of them—you.

Sedative

Hush, my dear, and let your hands
Wear stillness like a glove,
Or be like birds that fly to rest
And sing no song within the quiet
Of their nest.

Snow-on-the-Bush

The bush outside my window
Has grown old and overnight;
But awhile ago and it was green
And wearing bright red berries in flaming head-dress;
And it was young and blushed all summer
While the birds wooed in its arms;
And when the winds of autumn blew
It waved its arms and tossed its head and danced;
Yet this morning when I awoke
I looked and saw its head all streaked with white;
The bush outside my window
Has grown old and overnight.

Texas

The strength of oxen trudging through the wilderness,
The human tide of men advancing with their loves and
    lives
Into a land whose untamed spirit
Knew but calls of coyotes in the night
The swift and silent flash of Indian arrows
Darting after flying herds whose hooves beat out a song
A hundred years ago.

That song was heard
That promise was fulfilled:
Men saw a vision in the sunset fires
And brought that vision down to earth;
They worked for it and fought for it and died for it,
And as they passed they left behind
A vision even greater in sunset fires for other men
A hundred years ago.

Gone is that wilderness
But not the spirit whose home it was
For men still dream and men still build,
And cities are where camp-fires gleamed,
Cities where steel rings true on steel

And towers rear their gray stone heads
Where soaring engines cleave the sky like playthings
Of these children of a race that vanished
Only to return again inspired by growth to greater growth
A hundred years from now.

Eventide

There's something in twilight I love—
That mystic hour when
It is not day and
It is not night.
And the world is filled with soft gray light,
And shadows drift
Where shadows should—
It seems as if all the world is hushed and still
Waiting . . . waiting . . .

There's something about you at twilight
That I love—and fear—
That mystery of wondering if
It's really you that's here,
For the shadows drift about you
And you seem a part of all
That's going with the day
And coming with the night—
And I want to speak but somehow only sit and dream
Waiting . . . waiting . . .

Bedecked

Ah, my dear, before you go
Out for this night's revelry,
Come with me into this little room
And we will open my old jewel-box
All filled with gems long-saved
And waiting to be worn;
See, here is a necklace made of little kisses
Sparkling and on fire—needing only brushing up a bit
There, they glitter as they clasp your throat,
And should one ask you whence they came,
Say they are a many years' collection,
Well-matched, and picked by experts;
And here is a lover's knot to sport above your heart,
And for your hand a ring, a brilliant solitaire
Made of a great embrace and set in tender looks;
And on your hair wear this tiara
Shaped just like a heart —
Only a little broken, see, it does not show—
Ah, my dear, you look so lovely
Bedecked in my old jewelry.

Cherchez Les Femmes

The smell of sin
Is like perfume
To minds that hold it dear;
They pour it on from head to skirt
To spread the scent and make
Delectable their dirt.

In love they see adultery,
In friendship just psychiatry;
But in themselves they never see
Their own malignancy.

The Green Conscience

As long as his assistants had been working for Benjamin Lopez, they had never known him to be so bossy and cocky. Of course the business of handling the Farley funeral was a most definite and distinct feather in the cap of the Lopez Memorial Mortuary. It was going to be the biggest event in the Rio Grande Valley, and nobody had to pretend to feel sad about it because old Pete Farley was the richest man in ten counties and the meanest old son of a gun in the whole state. Everybody knew that, especially all the brothers and sisters and nieces and nephews flying and driving in from all over the country for this long-awaited occasion.

Some were staying out at the Farley ranch and some in town at the little hotel and motels. It was a real family reunion, and they were all as happy as larks to be this close at last to will-reading time. In anticipation they told Ben to shoot the works and spare no expense.

Accordingly he had ordered the most expensive casket available to be trucked down from San Antonio. He knew that old Farley would have thrown a fit, for no man ever roped a steer with as firm a grip as Farley had held on to his pocketbook. Folks said that was why he'd never married. Just too downright stingy to share even his own bed. Ben Lopez was no spendthrift himself. He had come up the long, hard way. As a wetback he had crossed the river at thirteen and gone to work for Pete Farley. He stole everything he could get his hands on, and Farley caught him at it and beat the devil out of him and turned him over to the priest.

Ben was a bright boy with a most distinguished and distinctive feature for a Mexican—the red hair of an Irish father who had been doing a bit of civil engineering south of Laredo. In his confession to the priest, Ben explained his misconduct was due to the fact that he had a green conscience, because the day he was born his father went out looking for a conscience for his son and never came back, not having been able to find one that was at all ripe yet. That was the story which Ben's mother had told him as a child, and what kind of a man was going to doubt his own mother?

Ben still told the story with a great deal of relish to justify himself when some of his actions were questioned or criticized for penny-pinching. At fifteen his peasant-plus sagacity had figured out that the only way to get anywhere was to learn a business to go into for himself. But what business? The more he thought about it, there seemed to be only two that were absolutely so necessary as to insure success. One was the business of getting people born, and the other the business of getting them buried.

Going to school long enough to learn to be a doctor to deliver babies was out of the question for him and so Ben went to work for the local undertaker, saved his money and ten years later took over the business when the owner went to whatever reward is in store for a man whose liver refuses to take another ounce of tequila.

Ben prospered. He had married a wife who was lovely enough to merit even a joint bank account. Twice a year he let her go all the way to Dallas to do her shopping. They already had twins, a boy and a girl. Another blessed event was fast approaching. There was also a new house which had cost several years' income in order to satisfy an expensive Houston architect's idea of the adobe style which Lopez ancestors had built for themselves without a peso. Ben was an American citizen, member of the Chamber of Commerce and Rotary, and at least one congressman called him "Ben."

Now with the Farley funeral it was no wonder that he was in such good spirits that when Father Martinez came to tell him that the old beggar Frank Yarby had finally died in the gutter where he had lived so long in alcoholic contentment, Ben graciously agreed to a funeral at his own expense. Of course nobody would come to it, but charity was good publicity. Ben had learned that too.

It was at just this most inopportune time that Rosa called to tell him to come home right away because she was beginning to feel as if she'd better get to the hospital as soon as possible. She was crying and that always scared Ben. It had taken a long time with the other babies and he had to stay right with Rosa and hold her hand to keep her from crying. Undoubtedly now he would have to miss attending to the Farley funeral himself. In frantic haste Ben checked over details with his assistants, José and Pedro. The main thing was to watch out for the arrival of that fabulous casket of course, and then Ben was off to his Rosa. He was nervous as any expectant father would be, and he was worried about having to leave matters of such importance with José and Pedro. Assistants were not trustworthy anymore. They didn't pay attention to what you told them. They thought they knew it all. They didn't care about anything except their Saturday night pay-checks and getting to be president of something.

If only Rosa would have this baby in a hurry.

She did not. It took forever. Thirty-six hours to be exact. And Ben never left her side nor let go her hand until he fainted dead away at the last moment just as he had done the time before. When he got back to his business two days later, he was the proud and happy father of another fine daughter. But he had missed the Farley funeral entirely. Evidently all had gone well.

As he parked his car and got out to go into his office, he met Father Martinez just going into the little chapel parlor. Ben went in with him, for after all somebody should attend poor old Frank's funeral. Ben sat down and prepared to listen to the priest, and then he stared in shocked horror. How could he believe his own eyes? Instead of the pine box that should be there, he saw the elaborate casket he had ordered for Farley. Those fools José and Pedro had ruined him. And there they sat in front of him, their idiotic heads bowed in prayer.

Ben started up, caught the Father's eye and sat down again. He got out pencil and paper began figuring. That made it worse, and nothing was deductible. He would fire them of course. But that wasn't enough. He would have them arrested, jailed, hanged. Surely there must be some law to prosecute persons for such stupidity. Finally the old priest was through and came down the aisle. He came right to Ben and put his arms around him.

"Bless you, my son! I always knew that in your heart you are a generous man, but not until now did I realize how generous! Not the rich man laid to rest here yesterday with all the flowers covering his casket, no, not even a prince was ever put away in such splendor as you gave this poor man. Bless you, my son, as you will be blessed. This will be my sermon Sunday, with your permission, of course."

Ben Lopez swallowed hard and nodded, not too eagerly he hoped. He was thinking fast, faster than he had added, divided, and subtracted. A huge smile began stretching across his face. He shook hands with José and Pedro. Maybe he would promote them to be his vice-presidents in charge of advertising. They had vision. No doubt of that. Ben was beaming like the noon-day sun over the Rio Grande as he walked out with the padre. He felt something very warm and big inside. It must be that new golden-ripe conscience he would be taking home to the little Chiquita.

Index